BECOME A
PROCEDURES
PRO™

Julie Perrine
CAP®-OM, MBTI® Certified,
Certified Productivity Pro® Consultant

Founder of All Things Admin
A Julie Perrine International, LLC Company

AllThingsAdmin.com
ProceduresPro.com

BECOME A
PROCEDURES
PRO™

The Admin's Guide to Developing Effective Office Systems and Procedures

Julie Perrine
CAP®-OM, MBTI® Certified, Certified Productivity Pro® Consultant

Founder of All Things Admin
A Julie Perrine International, LLC Company

AllThingsAdmin.com
ProceduresPro.com

Cover Design: Chris George
Cover Illustration: Sergey Myakishev

ISBN-10: 0982943091

ISBN-13: 9780982943090

Printed in the United States of America

10 9 8 7 6 5 4 3 2 1
First Paperback Edition

Dedication

This book is dedicated to all of the organized, innovative administrative professionals who put the effort and time into creating effective systems and procedures to keep their offices running smoothly!

Table of Contents

Foreword

It started with a tweet. We had recently relaunched Executive Secretary Magazine, and I was on the lookout for new authors. From the moment I saw Julie Perrine's tweet inviting administrative professionals to create their administrative procedures manual, I just knew. Here was our Procedures Queen. Julie has written for us ever since.

She began as an admin herself, and as she is fond of explaining when she speaks at conferences, she thinks she emerged from the womb organized. There is a particular slide that springs to mind, featuring a picture of Julie, age 2, already sitting next to the phone holding a three-ring binder.

Thinking her ability to create procedures was just something that every assistant does as standard, Julie was astonished to find that her administrative procedures binder template quickly became the stuff of legend – first within her own business and then via AllThingsAdmin.com. An unlikely superstar, Julie built her following and then an international business on how to instigate logical procedures and systems.

In this, her third book, Julie looks at both procedures and systems, explains the difference and the importance of both, and shows you how to implement them quickly and with minimal stress. Like Julie herself, the language is no-nonsense, to the point, and completely reliable. This is the book that you need to simplify the way your office runs whether you are present or not.

Julie brings order to everything she touches. Calm, efficient, and productivity-driven, her exceptional, but methodical, systems-driven brilliance has been adopted by assistants worldwide. She has literally changed lives by bringing order to chaos. Her systems, procedures, and productivity tools have added thousands of hours to the bottom line of corporate business across the world.

Executive Secretary Magazine is proud to have played a part in bringing Julie's techniques to a global audience both in person and virtually.

On behalf of the administrative profession and the millions of businesses that assistants serve, long may she continue.

Lucy Brazier
CEO, Marcham Publishing
Publisher of Executive Secretary Magazine
International Speaker, Conference Chair,
Expert on the Administrative Sector
ExecutiveSecretary.com

Introduction

*"My philosophy is that not only are you responsible
for your life, but doing the best at this moment puts
you in the best place for the next moment."*
~ OPRAH WINFREY

Procedures aren't just a project to tackle when you have some extra time. They are vital to an effective and efficient office. I know this firsthand.

I've held several administrative positions throughout my career, and not a single one had documented procedures when I started. So I made it my goal to create them as I was trained. This was an essential task, as procedures helped me deliver consistent work during my time at each job. I never left a company without leaving a binder full of procedures for my successors.

Fast-forward several years to January 2005 when I launched my virtual assistant business. Every small to mid-size company I took on as a client needed procedures. I helped entrepreneurs and established companies alike document and implement their procedures. In the summer of 2007, I began blogging about how to create procedures, and I realized a lot of people needed help with them. So I started creating templates, training, and tools to make the process easier.

However, it wasn't until January 2011 that procedures became very personal for me.

I was sitting at my kitchen table eating breakfast with my husband when my cell phone rang. The caller ID said it was my mom, but the voice on the other end was someone else's.

My mother had arrived at work early that day and slipped on the ice. Her coworkers found her in the parking lot when they arrived 30 minutes later. She was going into shock, and she had multiple injuries. I was told to notify my family and meet the ambulance at the emergency room as soon as possible.

My mother suffered multiple fractures and underwent a very delicate surgery to repair the damage from the fall. I spent most of the next two weeks working from her hospital room and much of the following three months working from her home an hour away from where I lived.

At the time, I was trying to finish my first book, and All Things Admin was just getting established in the admin training market. It was a very ambitious and hectic time for my company and career.

I called my accountant the week my mom fell to get her the information she needed for an annual filing. When I talked to her again three months later, it was time to prepare my taxes, and she sounded concerned. She asked how I was doing and how my business was doing. I said we were both doing fine. I shared that we hadn't launched any new products or broken any sales records, but things were functioning as close to normal as possible, given the situation. She looked at me with surprise and relief and asked, "How did you do it?" She was concerned when we spoke in January that my mom's accident would put me out of business. I told her there were two big reasons that didn't happen: established procedures and my team.

Since we have documented procedures for nearly everything we do, my team was able to keep things running smoothly while I was out. My colleagues were able to step in and do webinars using the procedures we had in place for delivering them. My team created and published our weekly newsletter. Everything was taken care of – even though I was only putting in a fraction of the hours I usually logged.

Fast-forward two years, and life struck again.

It was the end of August 2013. I had just finished a major client project that had drawn a lot of public scrutiny and media attention. It consumed a lot of my time, energy, and emotion for the previous 18 months. I was filled with relief and exhaustion when I turned off the lights and left the office that afternoon for the long holiday weekend.

The day before, my youngest sister had gone into labor with her first child. I knew I'd be receiving happy news at any minute as I drove home. Just knowing this helped to balance out the exhaustion.

But things did not go as planned.

My sister ran into complications that resulted in a record-setting labor and emergency surgery to deliver her baby girl. As I paced by the phone and clutched my iPad waiting for notification from anyone, I was preparing for the worst. Thankfully, my sister and her baby girl, Ellyana, both came through the surgery alive and healthy. But the impact this had on me physically, mentally, emotionally, and spiritually was profound.

Ten weeks later, my other sister went into labor…five weeks early.

Sadly, this time the outcome was tragic.

By a complete miracle, my sister survived the delivery, but her newborn daughter, Emma, died within an hour. It's still impossible to explain the tidal wave of emotions that hit me as I processed the news of the birth, and then the loss of my newborn niece shortly after. I felt like time stood still.

In between those two births, my grandfather died. My husband and I were traveling internationally when it happened, so we were unable to get home in time for his funeral. Then, three months later, my mother was diagnosed with breast cancer.

For much of the following six months, my company ran without me – once again, because of procedures and my team. This time, we were even more prepared, because we had filled some gaps that became evident during the previous experiences. I was able to step away from work, be present for my family, and take care of myself during one of the most stressful and awful periods of my life.

The following spring, my husband got a new job in Indianapolis. We moved from Iowa to Indiana during one of my busiest speaking seasons of the year. Within a month, my husband started a new job, we put our house up for sale, I coordinated the packing and moving details for a two-state move, and I traveled to several speaking engagements. Procedures and checklists kept life moving forward for me personally and professionally!

In January 2016, we learned that my mom's cancer had returned, and it had metastasized. We didn't know when the end would be, but we knew it was coming faster than any of us were prepared for. Five months later, my mother died. For several weeks, I could barely pull myself off of the couch, let alone run my business. I have never experienced such complete exhaustion, and I have never been more thankful for procedures and the support of my amazing team.

These are just my personal stories on the importance of procedures. I can recount multiple examples from several of my team members to illustrate the need for them, too.

The takeaway from all of these examples is that procedures are more than just a good idea. They are mission critical to helping you be successful and ready for whatever life throws at you.

My hope is this book will help you with the process of creating, implementing, and updating your procedures so you, too, can enjoy the benefits of this invaluable resource.

Getting Started With Systems and Procedures Documentation

"The secret of getting ahead is getting started."
~ Mark Twain

Welcome to *Become a Procedures Pro*! When I launched my blog in 2007, I wrote a three-part series on how to create an administrative procedures binder. I assumed most people knew how to do it. But I was looking for a good topic to start writing about, and I knew this one well. I shared some tips and templates for starting the process, and didn't think much about it.

A few months later, I was reviewing my website statistics, and the topic driving the most traffic each month was the three-part series on procedures development. When I realized a lot of people wanted help with this, I began writing more articles, creating training, and sharing templates to help assistants worldwide start their procedures.

Now, several years later, I'm proud to be referred to as the "procedures pro," and I'm eager to help you create and maintain your administrative procedures.

In this book, I will help you think about procedures in terms of systems, and explain:

- Why you, your company, and your team need procedures.

- The difference between systems and procedures, and why you need both.

- How to map out your systems.

- Best practices for developing effective procedures.

- How to ensure your office runs smoothly no matter what.

Resources, Files, and What I Use

Throughout this book, you'll find these four icons indicating success stories, additional resources, files, or ideas for that chapter. Since products and technologies often change, I don't want to list the specific product brands or names in print. Instead, I've posted links and pictures on our website at **ProceduresPro.com**, so you can always find the latest tools I use and recommend.

 The speech bubble icon indicates a **Success Story** from a fellow admin.

The file folder icon indicates a **File Download.**

 The mouse icon indicates a **Resource Alert.**

 The pushpin icon indicates **What I Use.**

My Writing Style

I tend to write in a conversational style. While I do believe in good grammar, correct punctuation, and complete sentences, there may be places where I stray a bit for emphasis. (My editing team usually keeps me in line.) I share this because I know how particular admins, myself included, can be about written materials. Proofing other people's documents is, after all, part of what we do for a living. That said, if you find an error that I should correct in future editions, please visit the Contact page at **ProceduresPro.com** and let me know.

Throughout this book, the terms admin, assistant, and administrative professional are used interchangeably to represent the hundreds of titles that comprise the administrative profession. No matter what your specific title may be, this book is for you. I also use the terms manager, executive, boss, supervisor, and team when referring to those you work with or report to, but I recognize that there are lots of titles for these people, too.

Let's Get Started!

Whether you are creating a procedures binder to complete an official performance review goal, or you're looking for some backup and support for the next time you are out of the office, procedures can reduce stress and improve efficiency in more ways than one!

When you are out of the office, it's nice to be missed. But it's also nice when things run smoothly while you're away so you don't return to a bunch of problems or unhandled business. Procedures help with this – and so much more!

Mapping out your systems and creating your administrative procedures can seem like an overwhelming endeavor if you're just getting started. This book is dedicated to helping you simplify the process and making the project a lot easier!

If you're ready, let's get started on your systems and procedures development!

Chapter 1
Procedures Make Good Business Sense

"What you do today can improve all of your tomorrows."
~ RALPH S. MARSTON JR., AMERICAN WRITER

As an assistant, you're entitled to time off just like anyone else in the office – but when it feels like your department will come to a screeching halt if you want or need a break, you're not quite as prepared as you need to be.

If an accident, illness, or family emergency were to pull you away from your job, could someone easily fill in for you? If the career opportunity of your dreams came knocking, could you take it without leaving your executive, successor, or company in a lurch? Are you prepared for disasters – natural or otherwise? Procedures can help with all of these things, and that's why they make such good business sense!

Business Continuity

Business continuity – the ability to continue operations, despite an incident or interruption – is something every administrative professional needs to prepare for.

I can tell you from personal experience that the last thing you want to do when a tragedy strikes is try to do your job or run your office from your cell phone or laptop. Procedures allow others to handle tasks in your absence, which can be an enormous relief during difficult times. As I shared in the introduction, I've had a few instances where procedures came to the rescue and allowed me to focus on important family situations – without worrying whether my company would suffer.

Procedures aren't just for emergency situations, though. They can also be extremely useful in keeping things running when you're sick or on vacation. Administrative procedures arm your colleagues with the information they need to cover for you successfully, and demonstrate your commitment to keeping the office running – regardless of what happens!

Disaster Planning and Recovery

Until you experience a natural disaster, you have no idea exactly how important and valuable it is to have documented procedures, contact lists, emergency contact numbers, client information, and vendor information compiled and ready to go.

In June 2008, I lived in Cedar Rapids, Iowa, and my city was literally under water. Several companies were seriously impacted, and not all of them survived the disaster. However, many were able to resume business fairly quickly thanks to disaster recovery and business continuity plans – also known as disaster recovery procedures.

This is just one example of how procedures have helped in a disaster situation, and I've heard countless similar stories from admins across the country. From fires to tornadoes to snow storms, procedures are one key component that can help you and your company recover more quickly from a disaster. This is why you need to create emergency disaster procedures if you don't already have them. If your company does have something in place, get a copy, review it, place it in your binder, and identify what you need to add for your own position, team, and department.

We'll go into greater detail on disaster planning procedures later in this book.

Succession Planning

Have you ever pursued a promotion or had a new job present itself unexpectedly? Procedures are essential if you want to be prepared for career advancement opportunities.

What about retirement? If you are planning to retire in the next few years, it is absolutely necessary for you to document your job with procedures now. Retirement is something you can plan for, so there is no excuse not to do this.

Procedures ensure that your business can continue if you are away from the office. They make it easier for someone to fill in for you, whether you're dealing with an emergency, out of town for a career development opportunity, or just taking a well-deserved break. Procedures make great business sense!

Success Story: "In my previous position, I was employed as a finance and customer service coordinator. My job responsibilities included front desk reception and triaging inquiries from visitors and callers.

Because I was only one of two administrative positions in the office, if I happened to be out at the same time as of our office manager, no other staff knew how to utilize our new phone system. And, although we had a strong core phone team, when someone left or was promoted, it required training a new staff member. The position also included several financial processes, which were time-sensitive and required step-by-step detail in order to ensure accuracy and prompt distribution of related paperwork.

After attending an online webinar regarding office procedure manuals, I knew this was exactly what had to be created. Once in place, the training and information would be consistent as well as easy to follow.

I prepared my first sample and took it to my boss. With some insight and input from her, the new hard copy desk manual was created, along with a phone-system specific PDF version to be distributed to the core backup phone team.

It turned out to be one of the best things I did for that position! When I included the project in my self-evaluation for my annual review, it really impressed our management team. I used it to train my replacement, and she has continued to update and refresh the manual as the processes and systems change. Each position in every office should have a procedures manual. It really does serve as a GPS for guiding people through what needs to be done when you are not around to direct them."

– Kemetia M.K. Foley, CAP-OM

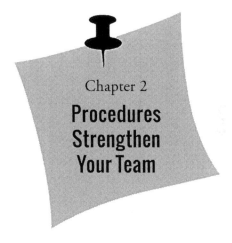

Chapter 2

Procedures Strengthen Your Team

"Do it now! Today will be yesterday tomorrow."
~ E.C. McKenzie, Author

I've already demonstrated how beneficial procedures were for me during some of the more trying times of my life, but procedures don't just benefit you as an individual – they also benefit and strengthen your entire team.

My team has procedures for just about everything we do, and this means we can all cover for each other when needed. My marketing director knows how to create the social media posts for the week; my social media assistant is fully capable of editing the monthly marketing brief, if necessary. When everyone is effectively cross-trained in every position through the use of procedures, we're a stronger, more capable team!

Procedures Help You Delegate More Effectively

When most people hear the word delegation, they think of handing off tasks to someone else. But there's so much more to delegation than that! When done properly, delegation keeps your office running smoothly. It allows everyone to function as a team, capitalizing on individual strengths, duties, and time management skills.

But for delegation to be effective, you need procedures. When someone requests your help with a task that you can't handle immediately or as soon as they'd like, you can offer an alternative by providing them with the procedure for how to do it. Then they can handle it themselves or find someone else to help them sooner. Procedures prevent you from wasting time trying to teach someone how to do a task. If you're inundated with work, you can hand off the task and the procedure for doing it, and use your time more productively while remaining confident that the task will get done correctly.

Procedures Put an End to Mission Creep

Has someone ever asked you to handle a task outside of your job duties, then never taken it back? Perhaps you covered for someone once, and somehow part of their job got transferred to you.

This is known as mission creep. It happens when you perform someone else's job duties for so long that no one (not even you) remembers that they're not your responsibility. Procedures can help you end this cycle once and for all!

Do your current duties match what you were hired to do, or what your executive expects you to do? Is there someone else in the office who has the time for some of the tasks that aren't really your responsibility? Create procedures for them, then delegate them!

Examples of these procedures include:

- Making coffee: Place this procedure in the break room, next to the coffee maker, so anyone can do it.

- Initiating a video conference: Leave a copy of this procedure on the conference room table so it's accessible for everyone.

- Feeding envelopes or labels through the printer: Post this procedure by the printer so staff can see how to do it when they need it.

You can do your tasks much more efficiently when you're not running yourself ragged for other people. It's nice to lend a helping hand when needed, but procedures cut down on unnecessary requests from co-workers who are more than capable of handling the task themselves.

Procedures Empower Others to Help Themselves

The old adage goes, "Give a person a fish, and they'll eat for a day; teach them to fish, and they'll eat for a lifetime." This applies to delegation and procedures, too!

Empowering your team through your procedures will ensure that they have the proper know-how to get the job done – rather than constantly asking someone else to do it for them. And in helping themselves, your co-workers are helping you, too.

Examples of these procedures include:

- Cutting checks or creating expense reports for team members or departments that you don't directly support

- Ordering company apparel or business cards through a website or intranet

- Accessing the intranet, HR site, or digital employee handbook

- Proofreading/style guide procedures to make it easier for employees to edit their own work

Most of the time, you'll find that your co-workers are willing to learn to do these things themselves, especially if it means they don't have to wait for you. They will be able to do their job faster and more efficiently thanks to documented procedures!

Procedures Give You a Backup Plan

Procedures are instrumental in creating your backup plan for coverage. Have you ever had to deal with an urgent request from your executive while trying to juggle all of your normal work? If you have documented procedures, you don't have to try to be in two places at once – you can simply ask for help. And those you ask for help will have a safety net when you have procedures documented for their reference.

Examples of these procedures include:

- Covering phones and front desk duties

- Preparing for and setting up a meeting (catering, conference room preparation, dial-in instructions for teleconferences or video conferences, etc.)

- Processing and sorting mail or packages

- Ordering supplies

- Handling travel arrangements for your executive or other senior officers

A tremendous amount of relief comes with knowing you can have someone perform some of your regular duties if you're pulled away due to a more urgent matter!

Procedures Provide Stress Relief for the Entire Team

Stress. We all experience it, and we're all constantly on the lookout for ways to alleviate it. But many people overlook one big way they can facilitate stress relief at the office: procedures. Procedures make everyone breathe a bit easier because everyone knows what's going on.

For instance, when my marketing director went on maternity leave, everything still functioned like clockwork – even though an integral member of the team was missing. I wasn't too concerned even before she left because I knew she had procedures in place. This reduced the stress for her, our teams, and me, and we were able to handle everything in her absence. That feeling of complete confidence in knowing things would run smoothly – even before she went on leave – was priceless!

Procedures are instrumental if you want to assure everyone on your team that things will continue to run – regardless of unexpected issues, emergencies, or who is or isn't in the office. In doing so, you will greatly reduce their stress levels… and your own!

Success Story: "I took the procedures course and loved it. I find that having my binder on hand has helped my work group tremendously. I went on an extended vacation to Italy, and I was gone for about three weeks. Upon my return, I found my binder on my desk (not my bookshelf), so I know it was used.

Later that week, we had our regular staff meeting, and at the beginning of the meeting we give kudos to other staff who have helped out. I received a resounding shout-out for my binder. Several people opened up about how useful they found it when looking for account codes, important phone numbers, and how to place toner orders. I told them I was very glad they found it so useful, and they all said, 'But don't go on another vacation.' It's nice to be missed!"

– Sharon K. Trnka, Executive Assistant

Chapter 3
Procedures Benefit Your Career

"Opportunities don't knock at all. They don't have to, they're already all around us. It's up to us to see where they are and take advantage of them."
~ DAVE THOMAS, FOUNDER OF WENDY'S FAST FOOD RESTAURANTS

P rocedures are a fantastic way to enrich and advance your administrative career. If you're on the fence about whether they're worth the time and effort, here are just a few of the ways in which they add value to your career, too.

Procedures Facilitate Your Ability to Lead

Executives need assistants who can see what needs to be done, and do it with little or no handholding required. Taking the initiative to create procedures is a great way to demonstrate your willingness to take the lead. I know this from personal experience!

Throughout my career, I've had many different administrative positions. None of the companies I worked for had a procedures manual when I started – but they did when I finished! I wasn't shy about sharing my manual with my executives, and they were always amazed that I had taken the initiative to create this invaluable tool. This simple action led other department heads to send their new admins to spend a few hours training with me during their first few days on the job. Because I had taken the initiative to create my procedures binder, I became recognized as an administrative leader within my company.

Procedures Serve as a Reference Tool and Ensure Consistency

Admins must manage a lot of information, details, forms, checklists, and data to do their jobs well. When you have a procedures manual, it's just as helpful to you as it is to others who may be covering for you when you're out!

Procedures also help you streamline and systemize your work. When you put things in print (even if that print is handwritten), it forces your mind to think things through in a logical order. You'll start to see where the inefficiencies lie, how to make certain tasks go more smoothly, and where natural batching can occur. You can improve your entire process – as you're writing the procedure!

Procedures Prepare You (and Others) for Opportunity

Life happens. Career opportunities show up, and when they do, you have to be ready. If you land a new position within your company or find a new job, the last thing you want to do is document your procedures. You likely won't have the energy, time, or enthusiasm to do it, and they won't be as complete as they need to be.

By creating your procedures now, you can save yourself the stress of having to rush to do them before you move on to bigger and better things. There are always going to be some last-minute things you need to wrap up when you move on, but procedures shouldn't be on that list.

Procedures Demonstrate Your Value and Responsibilities

Many executives know their assistants handle a lot for them and the rest of the team. But most of them would have a hard time filling a page with your specific tasks and activities. Your procedures binder is written proof of how valuable you are to your executive, team, and company.

It's also helpful when it's time for your annual performance review because you can use it to educate your executive, and showcase what you do each day, week, month, and year!

Procedures Are the Legacy You Leave Behind

Have you ever started a new job with only a few handwritten notes from your predecessor? If so, you can probably appreciate just how beneficial your administrative procedures will be for the next admin in your company!

Your administrative procedures are your legacy. Long after you've moved on to bigger and better things, they will remain as a testament to your initiative, devotion, and determination to better your office.

Procedures Allow You to Take Time Off

Even the most competent, dedicated admin is out of the office from time to time. Whether you're going on a well-deserved vacation, attending an out-of-town conference, or taking time off for an illness or family emergency, the fact remains: You're not there, and someone else needs to know how to do your job.

The solution? Procedures! Well-documented procedures – everything from how to reboot the copier to how to invoice a client – can erase the guilt and stress you feel being away from the office, ensure that your off time is really your own, and prevent you from coming back to a complete mess on your desk!

It's no secret that procedures take time to create – but maybe not quite as much time as you think! And the career benefit they offer is astronomical! I have yet to meet an assistant who regretted creating their administrative procedures.

Success Story: "I was preparing to go on medical leave and would be gone for at least eight weeks. At the time, I was supporting two busy senior officers and knew that anyone coming in to cover for me would be totally overwhelmed. So, to prevent that from happening, I started developing my administrative procedures binder. The person covering in my absence would have to hit the ground running, and this guide would serve as the tool to help them do it. Before leaving, I was able to spend a few days going over the binder with my temp. She was very appreciative to have such a detailed point of reference to help her quickly get up to speed. As a result, she felt more confident about covering for me. While out on leave, I would check on her periodically, and she would always comment on how helpful the binder had been to her. From a professional development perspective, my managers were blown away by my administrative procedures binder.

A few initiatives were developed out of the creation of this guide.

- I was asked to share my binder with the legal secretaries in my division in our Chicago and Washington, D.C. offices, and train them in how to create their own desk reference guide.

- At the completion of the first initiative, I will present the guide to other administrative staff in my association to get them on board.

- After I complete that initiative, I will revise my current guide to fit a general association standard for presentation to my HR division to possibly implement into a company standard for administrative personnel.

These initiatives are essentially goals for my Professional Development Plan, and each goal will be weighed and rated. Needless to say, this entire process has become very near and dear to me. A few of my direct manager's comments on my administrative procedures binder were:

'A very impressive piece of work!'

'I do not know of any document like it in the association. I'm going to suggest that each legal secretary in the legal and governance division prepare a similar desk reference manual for their positions.'

'The binder, which could potentially be used by all employees with secretarial functions throughout the association, demonstrated not only that she has a thorough understanding of her job duties, responsibilities, and performance expectations, but also that she is willing to share her knowledge with others for the benefit of the association.'

I am very pleased with the results and the many compliments I have received. It's a very rewarding feeling. I am excited to share with my colleagues this product and how it can make a difference for them in their professional development as it has done for me."

– Lá Shawn J. Sandifer, CAP

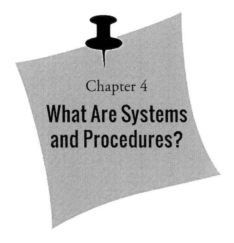

Chapter 4

What Are Systems and Procedures?

"There's a way to do it better – find it."
~ Thomas A. Edison

Systems and procedures are crucial to doing your admin job well. But while they're quite similar, they're not exactly the same. You have a procedure for processing an expense report; you have a system for doing the monthly accounting. A procedure is simply one component of a larger system, and most systems are made up of a series of procedures. However, simple systems can be made up of only one procedure.

Let's look at the difference between a system and a procedure, the components of each one, how they work together, and why you need them to be a more organized and efficient admin.

What Are Systems?

Whether you realize it or not, you probably have an established system for how you do repetitive tasks in your work. You have a system for how you get your day started, triage your email inbox, update your executive on changing priorities, and more. You have systems for planning events, organizing travel plans, and coordinating projects. Systems are one of the best methods for keeping yourself organized in your job and beyond!

Systems are ordered and proven processes that save you time, effort, and unnecessary stress. They are a set of instructions that create structure or govern actions. They make behaviors automatic so you don't have to think about them.

When it comes to setting yourself up for success, effective systems are at the heart of the equation. That's because systems are documentable, which makes them easy to share, transfer, and delegate. Systems are patterns for doing things that are repeatable. When systems are repeatable, they deliver consistent results over and over and facilitate business continuity.

So, what are the components of an effective system? Some key characteristics include:

- **Structure:** A documented system creates structure and outlines the pattern for how you get things done.

- **Behaviors:** Systems are a combination of behaviors or processes that interconnect.

- **Interconnectivity:** Systems have relationships and flow between the various actions that occur to make the system run effectively. Think of a flow chart where decisions occur and different procedures are initiated depending upon the decision made.

- **Boundaries:** Systems have a clear start and finish point. When you complete the cycle, you start over at the beginning and go through it again.

The tools you use to put effective and efficient systems in place include procedures, forms, templates, and checklists. (More on each of those later.) The good news is you're probably already using them in some capacity – it's just a matter of organizing them into systems to fit your specific objectives!

What Are Procedures?

A procedure is an established or official way of doing something that involves a series of actions conducted in a specific order. You probably have procedures for making coffee, ordering office supplies, and sorting incoming mail – even if you haven't written them down.

For more complex things, such as meeting planning, you likely have a series of procedures, forms, templates, and checklists. This is where you can see your individual procedures coming together to create your overall system for accomplishing something.

Almost every procedure you have fits into a larger system. Making the coffee may seem like a stand-alone procedure, but it's part of your office management system. The same thing applies to sorting mail and ordering office supplies. The procedures identify the step-by-step instructions for completing each task. The completed procedures become part of your overall system for office management.

No matter how simple or complex something is, documenting your procedures is an extremely important part of your admin job if you want to keep your office running smoothly and effectively support your executive and team.

The Benefits of Systems and Procedures

Systems and procedures are crucial to your success as an administrative professional because they enable you to provide consistent service, gain credibility, establish trust, and build confidence with those you support. Systems are also key in navigating change – both expected and unexpected – and help you course-correct more adeptly. And individual procedures provide great relief when someone else has to fill in for you.

Companies are always looking for ways to increase profitability. And, as an admin, you can play a direct role in helping your organization do that by documenting your processes and systems. Then you can engage your team in brainstorming ways to be more efficient. By increasing efficiency, you save both time and money, and as a result make your company more profitable.

Creating effective systems and procedures to support you and your team is vital to everyone's success.

 Success Story: "I wanted to have the peace of mind to know that I was doing everything I could to help train others in a clear and concise manner. I realized by documenting it myself, I'd be better able not only to train others to back me up when I'm on vacation, but also to onboard someone quickly if I needed to. Documenting procedures in the binder helped save me time by just having everything in one place. Finding things on my hard drive gets cumbersome.

This way I don't have to go and find the files again for a quick reference or to share with someone, and if I do, I know where to find them electronically by cross-referencing documents or checking the links at the bottom of a printed page. Before, I wasn't sure how or where to begin documenting. Now, I have a clear vision of what needs to be documented and can do it at my leisure in manageable chunks of time."

– S. L., Executive Assistant, San Diego, California

Chapter 5

Getting Started with Systems Development

"It always seems impossible until it's done."
~ NELSON MANDELA

Every office requires a different combination of systems to run efficiently. However, there are a few core systems I recommend most administrative professionals consider first, including:

- Time and Task Management
- Filing
- Travel Planning
- Meeting and Event Planning
- Project Management

In addition, you may need to consider some of these on your priority list:

- Disaster Recovery Planning
- Finance and Accounting
- Human Resources
- Customer Service
- Sales and Marketing

Once you have your top list of required systems identified, pick one. Try not to work on more than one at a time so you don't get overwhelmed.

Mapping Out Your Systems

The best way to explain how to document your systems on paper is to show you. Let's use meeting and event planning as our example, and focus on creating a system for planning quarterly board meetings.

Step 1: Brainstorm

Write down how you currently do it step-by-step.

When you're planning a board of directors meeting, what do you do and in what order?

1) Select date ranges or options for upcoming board meeting.

2) Check with all board members' assistants on availability for the ranges or options presented.

3) Determine preferred meeting date, time, and location with board chairman based on available options for all participants.

4) Determine who needs to attend in addition to current board members.

5) Determine the agenda and who is presenting.

6) Determine what types of audio-visual equipment you need.

7) Reserve the conference room.

8) Send out the board meeting invitation to all participants.

9) Determine whether there will be a board dinner the night before or after the meeting.

10) Determine date, time, and location of the board dinner.

11) Send out the dinner invitation to all participants.

12) Determine if board members need help with travel coordination for the meeting (hotels, flights, ground transportation).

13) Coordinate travel plans for those who request them.

14) Determine catering needs for the board meeting.

15) Order the catering for the board meeting.

16) Create the board meeting agenda for the chairman's approval.

17) Gather all board materials for the board books.

18) Create and/or assemble the board books.

Step 2: Think in Terms of Batching

Look for logical breaks in the process.

Date Selection

1) Select date ranges or options for upcoming board meeting.

2) Check with all board members' assistants on availability for the ranges or options presented.

3) Determine preferred meeting date, time, and location with board chairman based on available options for all participants.

Meeting Agenda and Attendees

4) Determine who needs to attend in addition to current board members.

5) Determine the agenda and who is presenting which topics.

Conference Room Logistics

6) Determine what types of audio-visual equipment you will need.

7) Reserve the conference room.

8) Send out the board meeting invitation to all participants.

Board Dinner Planning

9) Determine whether there will be a board dinner the night before or after the meeting.

10) Determine date, time, and location of the board dinner.

11) Send the dinner invitation to all participants.

Travel Planning

12) Determine if board members need help with travel coordination for the meeting (hotels, flights, ground transportation.)

13) Coordinate travel plans for those who request them.

Meeting Catering

14) Determine catering needs for the board meeting.

15) Order the catering for the board meeting.

Board Books

16) Create the board meeting agenda for the chairman's approval.

17) Gather all board materials for the board books.

18) Create and/or assemble the board books.

Step 3: Make It Visual

Color code, bold, italicize, highlight, draw lines and boxes.

This step is especially helpful if you're mapping your system out on paper first. But you can certainly color code, highlight, and draw boxes around things in digital documents to draw attention to them in print, too.

Date Selection

1) Select date ranges or options for upcoming board meeting.

2) Check with all board members' assistants on availability for the ranges or options.

3) Determine preferred meeting date, time, and location with board chairman based on available options for all participants.

Meeting Agenda and Attendees

4) Determine who needs to attend in addition to current board members.

5) Determine the agenda and who is presenting which topics.

Conference Room Logistics

6) Determine what types of audio-visual equipment you will need.

7) Reserve the conference room.

8) Send the board meeting invitation to all participants.

Board Dinner Planning

9) Determine whether there will be a board dinner the night before or after the meeting.

10) Determine date, time, and location of the board dinner.

11) Send the dinner invitation to all participants.

Travel Planning

12) Determine if board members need help with travel coordination for the meeting (hotels, flights, ground transportation.)

13) Coordinate travel plans for those who request them.

Meeting Catering

14) Determine catering needs for the board meeting.

15) Order the catering for the board meeting.

Board Books

16) Create the board meeting agenda for the chairman's approval.

17) Gather all board materials for the board books.

18) Create and/or assemble the board books.

Step 4: Make It Easy to Read/Scan

Use numbers for ordered lists and bullets for information.

I couldn't get through this meeting-planning example without numbering the items as I worked through it. But when I write things on paper first, I typically need to go back through my brain dump and number things so I get them in the right order.

Step 5: Test It Out

Continue to update your system as you use it.

The next time you plan a board meeting, follow your documented system, or have a colleague review it and test it out beforehand. That's the best way to know what is missing and figure out if it works the way it should. Update your system as you use it and discover other steps or tips you need to include to make it work even better.

Breaking Down a System Into Segments or Phases

In the second step of creating a system, I encouraged you to think of the system in terms of batches. These batches create the segments or phases of the system where you can supplement even further with forms, templates, checklists, and more detailed procedures, if needed.

Using the board meeting-planning example, here are the batches or segments:

- Date Selection

- Meeting Agenda and Attendees

- Conference Room Logistics

- Board Dinner Planning

- Travel Planning

- Meeting Catering

- Board Books

Identifying the Procedures for Each Phase

Now, let's identify where to use forms, templates, checklists, and more detailed procedures for each batch or segment on the list.

- Date Selection

    - Email template for initiating the process

    - Procedure explaining the nuances of board scheduling and working with other board members' assistants to pick the date

- Meeting Agenda and Attendees
    - Meeting agenda template
    - Meeting invite/email template
    - Procedure explaining how to determine the agenda and extra participants
- Conference Room Logistics
    - Procedure for conference room reservations
- Board Dinner Planning
    - Board dinner planning form
    - Procedure explaining board dinner scheduling
- Travel Planning
    - Travel profile form for each traveler
    - Travel planning form for travel arranging
    - Travel itinerary template
    - Procedure explaining the nuances of board travel planning
- Meeting Catering
    - Catering order form
    - Procedure explaining catering preferences

- Board Books
    - Board book PowerPoint template
    - Procedure explaining the board packet assembly and distribution process for each board meeting

Once you create your list, now it's time to start working on the procedures you need to fully document your system.

Success Story: "Faster responses, consistent communications, and efficient workflow are the primary outcomes of creating procedures to operate my business as a sole proprietor. As a solopreneur providing virtual assistant (VA) services for multiple small business owners daily, utilizing standard operating procedures to facilitate work in my own business is paramount. I routinely refer to my operations manual where my procedures are stored. Thanks to the proficiency that creating procedures has afforded me, I can develop an operations manual for my clients, incorporating instructions for tasks I perform for them, as a guide and resource to build as their business grows."

– Melissa St. Clair, owner of Paper Chaser

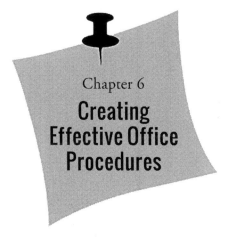

Chapter 6

Creating Effective Office Procedures

"The will to succeed is important, but what's more important is the will to prepare."
~ BOBBY KNIGHT, BASKETBALL COACH

Many admins cringe when they think about creating an administrative procedures binder. Where in the world do you begin when it feels like you are responsible for everything that happens in your office? How do you put on paper what you actually do?

While this project may seem overwhelming, it doesn't have to be. The secret is breaking it down into simple steps and approaching them one at a time.

The following are my five simple steps to starting your administrative procedures binder and populating it with the procedures to keep your office running smoothly.

Five Simple Steps for Creating Your Procedures

Here are the five simple steps:

Step 1: Assemble the Right Tools for the Job

Step 2: Track Your Tasks for a Few Days

Step 3: Document Your Top Five Procedures

Step 4: Identify What to Include in Your Procedures Binder

Step 5: Organize Your Procedures Binder for Ongoing Use and Success

Now let's examine each one individually.

Step 1: Assemble the Right Tools for the Job

To get your procedures binder started, gather a few basic office supplies:

- A three-ring binder, preferably one with an extended cover so your tabs are protected.

- A couple sets of tabbed sheet protectors for section dividers.

- A stack of sheet protectors for preserving frequently used pages. (Note: Sheet protectors aren't necessary for most procedures as they make it more difficult to update information.)

What I Use: Visit **ProceduresPro.com** to find links to products I use in creating my procedures binders.

Once you have these items, create a binder cover and spine label that identifies the contents of the binder. Feel free to have some fun naming it and creating the cover! Your binder should make you smile and encourage you to keep working on your procedures every time you look at it. Get creative, include images and colors that inspire you, and enjoy the process! You can always create a more polished and professional one for use once you have it completed. The bottom line here is you want this binder to be easily identified no matter where it lives on your desk.

 File Download: Download a sample cover and spine to get your procedures binder started at **ProceduresPro.com**.

Next, create a generic table of contents that includes a list of sections you anticipate you'll need as a starting point, and the order you want them in. You'll spend more time finalizing the sections in Step 5, so don't overthink this. Just create a list to get you started. Some sections to consider include:

- Accounting

- Facilities

- Event / Meeting Planning

- Executive-specific Information

- Catering / Menu Planning

- Contacts

- Daily / Weekly / Monthly Checklists

- Projects

- Office Supplies

Finally, create a permanent home for this binder on your desk so it is easily accessible. You should be able to reach your binder when you are seated at your desk in front of your computer and phone. It needs to be within arm's reach whenever you need it – not up on a shelf or stored in a file drawer away from where you work.

Step 2: Track Your Tasks for a Few Days

You may already have a list of some obvious things you need to include in your procedures binder. However, you likely do a lot of things each day that you take for granted, but that others may need to know in your absence. The best way to identify those not-so-obvious procedures is to track your time and tasks for a few days.

To get started, make a list of your specific job responsibilities and how often you handle them (daily, weekly, monthly, quarterly, annually, as needed). Next, create a list for each manager you specifically support and identify the types of recurring meetings, events, or items that you handle for each person (daily, weekly, monthly, quarterly, annually). Whether you use the spreadsheet template provided or a pen and notepad to track your tasks, it doesn't matter. The goal is to log everything you do from the moment you walk in the door in the morning until you leave at night.

I recommend you track your tasks for up to a week so you capture as much of your normal routine as possible. You can keep adding to it from there. The first week of tracking gives you an excellent starting point for prioritizing which procedures you need so you can start creating them.

As you write down your tasks, note when they're typically done (day of week and time of day). Once you dive in, you'll probably be surprised at how many procedures already exist in various formats that you can quickly insert into your binder.

File Download: Download a free template to help you track your tasks on our website at **ProceduresPro.com**.

Step 3: Document Your Top Five Procedures

In my experience, the secret to successfully creating your procedures is to work on no more than five at a time. That's one procedure per day for a workweek – it's manageable and motivating. So, pick your top five procedures and start documenting them.

Which five should you choose first?

- If you are the sole person who handles certain critical procedures for your team, and this keeps you up at night, *identify the five most critical* procedures and document them first.

- If speed is a motivating factor for you, and you want to gain some positive momentum early in this process, *choose the five fastest* procedures you can document and do them first.

Keep in mind, your procedures binder doesn't have to be perfectly formatted; it just needs to be functional and available to the people who may need it in your absence. Five documented procedures are five documented procedures – no matter how they look! They can even be handwritten. The goal is for someone to get from the start to the finish. If they can read your handwriting, that works! Plus, if you use the procedures template we provide, they'll have some consistency and structure built into them until you have time to type them out.

The Anatomy of a Procedure

So, how do you create an effective procedure? Here are a few key things to keep in mind:

- **Use a template for consistency.** Using a template to capture your handwritten procedures can help keep them structured and consistent, especially if you don't have time to type them immediately. Once you have a template, print out several blank copies, punch three holes in each page, and keep them in a file folder within arm's reach. Then you can grab a form and create a procedure any time you think of a new one.

File Download: Download a sample procedures template to help you get started at **ProceduresPro.com**.

- **Go through each task or process step by step.** As you create your procedure, think about each step you take to complete it. Write the steps down much like you would an outline. Then go back and fill in the details or background information where appropriate.

- **Think commands, not sentences.** You want to be specific without being excessively wordy. This is not a college research paper; it's a procedures binder. People are more likely to read simple commands than complete sentences, especially if they are in a hurry. And important information can get lost in a large block of text.

- **Use bullets or numbers as much as possible.** Number the steps that need to be completed in a specific order. Use bulleted lists for non-order-specific instructions.

- **Provide screenshots for computer-related tasks.** To make your procedures even more effective, create a graphic or visual (such as a screenshot) of computer-related tasks to accompany the printed or written instructions.

- **Ask another person to test your procedures.** The best way to know if your procedures will work is to have someone else test them. Ask them to point out items that don't make sense and list any questions they have about the procedures. This will help you identify gaps and fix them.

File Download: Download an infographic at **ProceduresPro.com** to keep these tips visible as you create your procedures.

To help you better understand what an effective procedure looks like, here's an example of a mail sorting procedure from two different administrative procedures binders at two different companies. Sometimes procedures are very basic, like the first one. Others are more detailed, as in the second example. While they're different, both are acceptable.

Example 1: Sorting the Incoming Mail

- All incoming bills, bank statements, invoices, and payments – route to accounting.

- All incoming trade magazines and trade show flyers – route to sales and marketing.

- All incoming resumes and interview thank you notes – route to HR.

- All incoming contracts – route to legal.

- Any office equipment or office supply mail – leave in my inbox.

Example 2: Sorting the Incoming Mail

Contracts

- Photocopy the incoming contract.

- Three-hole punch the photocopied contract and put them in the executed contracts binder on [name of person's] third bookshelf inside her office door.

- Forward the original contract to [name of person] in legal.

- If you have any questions regarding contract routing, contact [name of person] at [phone number] or [email address].

Bank Statements

- Open the envelope.

- Stamp the statement with the date received stamp.

- Forward the statement to [name of person] in accounting.

- If you have any questions regarding bank statement routing, contact [name of person] at [phone number] or [email address].

Trade Publication, Trade Show Flyers, or Marketing-Related Mail

- Forward to [name of person] in marketing.

Invoices (Accounts Payable)

- Open the envelope.

- Stamp the invoice with the date received stamp.

- If it's an office supply or equipment-related invoice, verify that the amounts and charges match what you anticipated for the month. Refer to the office supplies folder to match my individual order confirmations with the monthly statement.

- Initial the amount.

- Forward to [name of person] in accounting.

- If you have any questions regarding accounts payable routing, contact [name of person] at [phone number] or [email address].

For every section of the mail sorting procedures shown, the last bullet is probably the most important. You know who you call every day when you have a question, but if someone else is sitting at your desk, they may not have that information. It's important to tell the person filling in for you who else might be a good resource if you don't have enough detail in your procedures.

 What I Use: View more sample procedures my team uses at **ProceduresPro.com**.

Creating effective procedures isn't complicated, especially once you get into the habit of documenting each task. Don't overwhelm yourself by trying to document each and every procedure in a single week. Instead, strive to tackle five at a time. If it takes you all week, that's fine. If you can achieve it in a day, even better. Keep yourself motivated and moving forward by simply focusing on five at a time!

Step 4: Identify What to Include in Your Procedures Binder

In addition to the list of tasks you start tracking in Step 2, think about what procedures may already be documented for your position that you can include in the binder. This is one way you can fast-track the procedures development process.

- Start by reviewing your job description. Even if it's out of date, it may trigger some ideas of what else you need to include or things you may have documented from when you first started in your position. And when you're finished with this project, you'll have a comprehensive list to share with your executive to build the business case for updating your job description and possibly your job title as well.

- Consult with other administrative professionals within your company to see what procedures they have created.

- Check with internal departments – such as the mailroom, facilities, accounting, and human resources – for procedures that are standard across the entire company.

- Ask your IT department or do an internet search for procedures on how to use web conferencing tools, voicemail, and other office technology.

Many routine office procedures are likely similar from desk to desk at your company, so don't go it alone or try to reinvent the wheel. Partner with your colleagues to maximize everyone's efforts.

Here are just a few ideas to get you brainstorming on other procedures you may want to include:

- Handling basic office operations, such as transferring phone calls, routing mail, and making the coffee

- Information or resources you refer to regularly, including organizational charts, facility maps, phone lists, and branding standards

- Details about recurring events or meetings you coordinate

- Phone, computer, and video conferencing system user guides

- Department, manager, or project specific information

- Checklists, forms, and templates

- Disaster recovery or business continuity plans

- Sending department- or company-wide emails (e.g., Do you have a standard email template? Does someone have to approve it before you hit send?)

- Morning/opening tasks

- Evening/closing tasks

- Filing electronic and paper documents

- Supply storage locations and ordering supplies
- Proofreading tips and style sheets

Think about what information and resources you refer to on a regular basis:

- Phone lists (for vendors, internal departments, and individuals)
- Conference room locations and phone numbers
- Facility maps
- Org charts and executive/board contact sheets
- Travel planning forms
- Event planning checklists
- Corporate logo/branding guidelines
- Accounting codes or cost center information
- Shipping information
- Processing reports

Consider what forms or templates you use regularly: fax cover sheets, accounting, travel, event planning, HR, shipping, corporate PowerPoint presentations. Keep a few blank copies in your admin binder for quick access, just in case of computer or power failure.

If you need to motivate yourself, start by pulling together the "quick hit" items on your brainstorming list first. Then go back and chip away at the procedures on your top five list. Or complete the quick hits in between the procedures on your top five list. The primary goal is to add at least five procedures to your binder each week.

How to Handle Confidential information

As admins, we have access to a lot of confidential information; it's part of doing our job. The key here is not to have it openly accessible to anyone walking by your desk who could pick up your administrative procedures binder. For confidentiality and security, some key pieces of information should not be stored in your procedures binder. These items can include:

- **Passwords.** It's important to know your corporate policies on sharing passwords. If you do need to write down password documentation, keep it in a separate file in a locked drawer. You may also want to keep one password-protected spreadsheet saved on your computer in a shared area where both you and your executive can access the information.

- **Credit Card and Banking Information**

- **Personal and Government IDs, Passport Numbers, and Driver's License Numbers**

- **Dates of Birth**

The following are some tips for maintaining this confidential information:

- Keep a brightly colored file folder for each executive or team you support that is labeled – "Admin Info for Executive Name" or "Executive Name – Admin Info."

- Place this file at the back of a file drawer that is locked when you're out, your area is unattended, or after hours.

- Make sure your executive (or the appropriate person) has a key and knows how to access this information if you are out of the office.

Step 5: Organize Your Procedures Binder for Ongoing Use and Success

Once you have the majority of your procedures documentation complete, it's time to organize your binder for ongoing use. Start by finalizing the tabbed sections you will include.

Create a table of contents and a clearly labeled sheet for each tabbed sheet protector. You may want to list the section (e.g., Accounting), and a bulleted list of the procedures that are included in that section (e.g., processing check requests, submitting expense reports, etc.).

If you notice a particular section is getting bulky, evaluate if you need to break it down into additional sections to keep the information more manageable. For example, Event Planning may need to be broken down into Catering, Onsite Meetings, and Offsite Meetings.

As you organize and evaluate your print documentation, it's a good time to think about which digital storage tool makes the most sense for you and the users who will need access to this information. There are a lot of digital options including:

- Shared Network File Directory
- SharePoint Site

- OneNote Notebook
- Cloud-Based File Server

 Resource Alert: To view examples of some of these digital storage options, visit **ProceduresPro.com**.

The goal is to only have one digital copy stored in one location so you always know where the most current files are. You don't want multiple copies in multiple locations or you'll end up needing a procedure for updating your procedures, which is a waste of your time. You'll need to take into consideration the security options available to you with each option. Do you want people to have read-only access? Or are they allowed to open and edit the procedures as they use them?

If you choose a shared network folder or cloud-based storage tool, create a folder called "Admin Procedures Binder" for ease in filing these documents once they're in electronic format. Then create a sub-folder for each tab of your binder so it's easy to find what you're looking for in either the print or the digital version. Also add the document path and file name to the footer of each document before you print it. This will help you track the file down again later if you can't remember where you saved it. Create a desktop shortcut to the folder location on your computer for ease of adding and updating information as you think of it.

Once you create your procedures binder, update it regularly. Don't waste your time and effort to develop it only to let it get outdated. As you use it, write notes in your binder on the pages that need updates. If you have time to update it on the spot, do it. If you don't, come back and do it when you see you have several marked-up pages. Review it on a monthly or quarterly basis (at a minimum), depending on how busy your office is and how frequently changes occur. It's also helpful to set a recurring reminder in your calendar so you don't forget.

Once you complete this valuable tool, share the materials with your executive(s) and those who might have to cover for you. Invite these people to preview it before your next scheduled absence. Ask them if they have any questions or need additional information. Make sure they know where the binder lives on your desk. It may take a little time for everyone to get used to having something to refer to while you're away. Just keep reminding them that the tool was created for their use, too.

It's also a good idea to check up with the person who covered for you when you get back to the office. Their feedback about what worked (and what didn't) can be valuable information as you make improvements in your binder.

Success Story: "This started out as 'I need to brush up on my skills and organize myself for training,' but quickly turned into 'OMG, this process will positively alter my business.' I keep too much in my head and it blocks others from stepping into their gifts. This is a process that I will use over and over again to help others utilize their gifts and succeed!"

– J. Conner, Administrative Professional

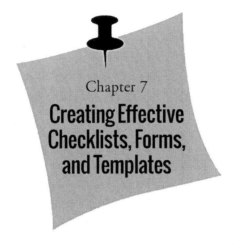

Chapter 7

Creating Effective Checklists, Forms, and Templates

"Do your work with your whole heart, and you will succeed – there's so little competition."
~ Elbert Hubbard, American Writer and Philosopher

Forms, templates, and checklists are effective ways of supplementing your written procedures. They help organize large quantities of details and information in a logical and straightforward manner that is easy for you and other users to navigate quickly when needed.

Creating and Using Effective Checklists

Admins have been using checklists for years, but are you using them enough? You might think, "Oh, that's not that important" or "I'll remember that." But this isn't the best mindset! Get the details on paper, place the paper in your procedures binder, and stop trying to remember all of this stuff. You need to clear that headspace for more important things, like coming up with innovative solutions to challenges and projects, and thinking about what you're doing and why.

The following is a sample of my new employee office supply checklist. It contains everything you need to inventory in a new employee's office or workspace so you can locate or order any missing items prior to their start date. It's simple, yet it ensures you remember these items for all new hires.

New Employee Office Supply Checklist

- ❑ Desk caddy
- ❑ Highlighter
- ❑ Mousepad
- ❑ Notepad
- ❑ Paperclips
- ❑ Pens
- ❑ Phone list
- ❑ Phone operation booklet/instructions
- ❑ Post-it pads in various sizes
- ❑ Push pins
- ❑ Scissors
- ❑ Stapler

❑ Tape

❑ Tape dispenser

❑ Telephone directory

❑ Wastebasket

Here is a checklist I created to keep me on track when I was working as an office manager. It includes to-dos for the beginning, middle, and end of the day, as well as weekly and monthly tasks.

Beginning of the Day

❑ Unlock doors.

❑ Turn off forwarding on phones.

❑ Check voice messages.

❑ Log into PC.

❑ Read emails.

❑ Check/review today's calendars for (executive's name).

❑ Check tickler (bring-back) files.

❑ Pick up notes/mail from weekend.

❑ Review in-tray items that came overnight/over the weekend.

❑ Turn copier on.

❑ Turn lamp/light on.

❑ Meet with (executive's/manager's name) to review day's priorities.

During the Day

❑ Answer phones.

❑ Check, prioritize, and respond to email.

❑ Sort, open, and respond to mail.

❑ Greet and direct visitors.

❑ Work on/complete projects.

End of the Day

❑ 3 p.m. – Check with (executive's/manager's name) to see what we need to get done before the end of the day.

❑ Review tomorrow's projects/tasks.

❑ Review (executive's name)'s calendars for next day.

❑ Clear out inbox tray.

❑ 4:30 p.m. – Print (executive's name)'s daily calendar page for the next day. (On Friday, also print a week-at-a-glance page for the next week.)

❑ Clear off desktop.

❑ Lock file drawers.

- ❏ Turn off coffee pot.
- ❏ 5 p.m. – Forward phone, log out of computer, and turn off copier.
- ❏ Turn off lamp/light.
- ❏ Lock front door.

Weekly Items

- ❏ Water plants (lobby, executive's office).
- ❏ Email kitchen cleaning schedule reminders and follow-up.
- ❏ Order/purchase office supplies.
- ❏ Stock water for executive's guests.
- ❏ Create weekly team in/out schedule and post on the bulletin board.

Monthly Items

- ❏ Email cleaning/dusting schedule reminders and follow-up.
- ❏ Recycle office paper.

While a lot of these things might seem like second nature, it's easy to forget something when you're having a particularly busy or stressful day at the office. And including this information in your procedures binder means someone filling in for you (who doesn't generally perform these tasks) won't overlook anything. I used to keep this checklist on a bulletin board next to my computer monitor so I could quickly reference it to ensure I'd done the basics each day. Not having to remember all of these things allowed me to better focus on the day's priorities and not worry about forgetting something.

These are just a couple instances of checklists you can create and use in your job. However, there many other areas in which a checklist can be helpful – from setting up for a board meeting to helping your executive prepare for travel. I strongly encourage you to put this simple but extremely useful admin tool to work for you!

Creating and Using Effective Forms

While checklists help you remember tasks and other to-dos, forms create a logical and orderly flow to information that needs to be collected or shared. And they are crucial in keeping you prepared!

To create a form, think about all of the information you need to collect for a task or project. Then capture and organize it in a logical way so you're able to efficiently get the right information when you need it.

At one company I worked for, I was responsible for ordering business cards and logo apparel for new employees. I needed the same information every single time, so creating a standard form that new employees could fill out was the most efficient for both of us. It ensured I got the right information and submitted the order properly every single time.

I did the same thing with meeting and event planning procedures. Each meeting required me to figure out the same details, so I created a standard form to use as a planning guide.

The purpose of these forms is to make them easy to navigate by using a method called information mapping. Information mapping creates a systematic approach to organizing and presenting information so readers can easily access, understand, and act on it.[1] Headings or section titles are listed on the left side and the corresponding data on the right. The cells of data on the right side can then be formatted using bullets or numbers. Typically, documents are formatted using a table so you can order things with rows and columns. Using this method for meeting and event planning forms works well because you can quickly scan a long form and locate the exact information you need.

 File Download: Download a sample Meeting Planning Form at **ProceduresPro.com** that uses information mapping to organize the details.

When your executive starts giving you notes on meeting arrangements, you can grab your form and capture the important information immediately. And you'll probably get more of what you need from your executive up front because your form will remind you of what to ask for. That's the magic and beauty of creating an effective form!

How and When to Create a Template

If you get tired of editing the same things in the documents you proof, templates could be your new best friend. Templates help you and others you work with maintain a consistent and professional look from document to document. And they're essential tools for assistants because they keep you consistent from document to document.

A template is a format for a document or file you set up so you can use it again and again. If you have a digital letterhead, memorandum, presentation slides, standard report, or meeting agenda that you regularly use, it's probably a template. With a template, you can quickly and easily create new documents based on the template because it contains all of the formatting, fonts, headers, footers, layouts, and style elements you need.

A template is useful for anything you want to maintain consistent standards for formatting, styles, etc. Some types of templates you may want to create include:

- Business letterhead

- Memos or emails

- Meeting agendas

- Standard reports

- Procedures templates

- Travel itineraries

 File Download: Download a sample travel itinerary at **ProceduresPro.com**.

Programs for Creating Forms, Templates, and Checklists

I'm often asked my opinion on the best software program for creating a form, template, or checklist. I recommend several.

Microsoft Word is one of the simplest tools to use for form/template/checklist creation because almost everyone has it. Adobe Acrobat Pro can be a good tool if you learn how to use all of the ins and outs of the software. Microsoft Excel is also a good tool depending on the form's or template's functionality. But every software program you use likely has an option for creating a template to base future documents on. You just have to explore the software and/or get some training on it so you know how to use it effectively.

Success Story: "Before implementing the administrative procedures binder, I relied on my memory and the memory of my co-workers to complete duties when someone (including me) was absent. Now, I feel confident that the needs of my boss and my 'customers' will be met in my absence."

– Terri Plank, Spoughton, Wisconsin

Chapter 8

Disaster Planning and Recovery

"By failing to prepare, you are preparing to fail."
~ BENJAMIN FRANKLIN

What would you do if you had just hours or even minutes to evacuate from your office? Does your company have a disaster recovery or business continuity plan?

Hurricanes, fires, flood, and other disasters usually don't come with much warning, and most small- and mid-size businesses are dramatically unprepared for disasters.

- Almost 40% of small businesses never reopen their doors following a disaster, according to FEMA.[2]

- 75% of small businesses do not have a disaster recovery plan in place, according to a 2015 survey by Nationwide.[3]

- 51% of businesses surveyed in the 2014 Disaster Recovery Preparedness Benchmark Survey received a failing grade.[4]

Disasters are not always the result of Mother Nature either. According to Infrascale, 95% of businesses experience outages for reasons unrelated to natural disasters.[5] Power outages, gas leaks, technology failures, equipment malfunctions, cyber security breaches, and terrorist attacks are just a handful of the scenarios that companies need to proactively prepare for.

So how do you prepare to deal with a crisis?

The answer is to create your disaster planning and recovery procedures.

Most admins assume that someone else – HR, management, a different department, or other team members – are responsible for their company's disaster planning. But you have a core role in your office's day-to-day operations, which means you are in a unique position to add incredible insight and value to your company's disaster recovery plan.

The following simple steps will help you start creating a custom disaster recovery P.L.A.N. that includes your procedures:

- Prepare Your Procedures.

- Lists. Lists. Lists.

- Ask Questions. Ask for Information and Feedback.

- Network With Others.

Prepare Your Procedures

In an emergency, procedures are extremely valuable because they allow others to step in and help you keep the office running. Plus, they relieve you of the pressure of remembering every detail amid a chaotic situation.

You should think about contingency procedures for what to do in the event of a fire, water damage, or a power loss since each scenario requires a different response or procedure.

 Resource Alert: Visit **ProceduresPro.com** for templates to get you started documenting your disaster recovery procedures.

Keep a printed copy of your office procedures in a safe place at the office, and another copy in your home, and have a digital copy you can access remotely – that way you can get to your procedures no matter where you are. (Power and internet outages can keep you from your digital version, which is why a paper backup is important.)

Lists. Lists. Lists.

Lists are vital in an emergency. You'll need quick and immediate access to lists of information, including:

- Emergency contacts, including company executives, team members, maintenance crews, and security personnel

- Key vendors or suppliers

- Key customers
- Vital files, paperwork, equipment, and machines you need to work remotely

Ask Questions. Ask for Information and Feedback.

If you haven't already done so, ask for a copy of your company's disaster recovery plan. Read it and familiarize yourself with it. If you have questions, ask them. You might identify gaps that should be addressed. Don't be afraid to speak up. Even if the plan covers all of the major areas, think about what might be helpful to include for your team or department.

After you've created the procedures and lists for your plan, share the plan with team members and get their feedback on how to make it more complete. Once you get things rolling, stick with it until you complete the plan. Then make sure everyone on your team knows the procedures exist and how to access the information in case of an emergency.

Network With Others

When it comes to disasters, you can learn a lot from other admins, clients, and other professional connections. If you know people who have dealt with a disaster, ask them what they learned and whether they have advice for dealing with similar situations. Find out what information was the most helpful when the crisis hit and in the days and weeks that followed. You can even poll your network on social media for advice.

Disasters come in all forms and levels of severity, and each one requires a different type of response. It's probably not possible to come up with every imaginable scenario, but figuring out some potential scenarios will better prepare you for the unexpected. You'll also find a lot of common elements exist across your procedures and lists that you'll need regardless of the situation. When you have your procedures and other key documents ready at a moment's notice, you can react in a more coordinated fashion, get resources mobilized quickly, and manage the response effort effectively.

Success Story: "I live in Ft. Lauderdale and my office was evacuated due to Hurricane Matthew. I just wanted to share that as I awaited the hurricane, working from home, I had my admin procedures binder and my admin emergency kit close by! Thanks to you!"

– Janice Chizmar, Administrative Professional

What to Include in Your Office Emergency Kit

Your emergency kit is a key component in your disaster recovery plan. To help you compile your kit and lists, and ensure you don't forget anything, here's a handy checklist to help you get started.

Items to include on your office evacuation list:

- Laptop or hard drive and power cords

- Cell phone and power cord

- Procedures binder and confidential files you maintain for your executive with credit card numbers, Social Security numbers, passport information, and logins/passwords, etc.

- Key company files and contact lists

- Printed Outlook or email contacts (do this monthly or quarterly) for yourself and your executive

- Key client files and contact lists

- Key project files and contact lists

- Key vendor files and contact lists

- One-of-a-kind supplies or equipment you can't easily replace at an office supply store or that are absolutely vital to your daily operations

Key items you need to work successfully from a remote location, such as home or a hotel:

- Computer

- Phone

- Internet (MiFi devices are great options here also)

- Portable wireless printer

- Office supplies, including pens, pencils, notebooks, folders, etc.

- Electronic file access (either to your company server or to a cloud-based service)

Items your team will need immediately after an incident:

- Extension cords

- Power strips

- Flashlights

- Batteries (all types)

- Notepads

- Pens

- Post-It Notes

- Highlighters

- Tape, including duct tape, shipping tape, and regular tape
- Staplers and staples
- Paperclips and binder clips
- Envelopes – all sizes
- Printer ink/toner for portable printers

An emergency kit could be your office's saving grace during a disaster. Keep your box or boxes of emergency items, along with your lists, in a safe place close to your desk. Then if something happens, you can throw the items on your lists into the box and be ready to get out quickly.

Chapter 9

A Smooth-Running Office

"Systems allow you to create an office that functions smoothly, efficiently, and effectively...no matter what happens."
~Julie Perrine

The ultimate goal of creating effective systems and procedures is to ensure a smooth-running office no matter what happens. They provide stability for your team. They automate office operations. They help you provide consistent results over and over again. When you push through the initial development and implementation, the benefits begin to speak for themselves!

Troubleshooting a System

As wonderful as established systems and procedures can be, we all know how quickly things can change. You may find yourself struggling with something that you had a good system for, but now it's just not working. This happens.

When you notice the tension and frustration building, it's important to evaluate the system – not abandon it entirely.

When your system breaks, here are the steps you should take:

1. Troubleshoot it. Is it one piece that isn't working or the entire system?

2. Seek input from others. Sometimes, having someone else help you troubleshoot your system makes it easier to pinpoint and resolve the problem.

3. Write down what would work better. Then test it.

4. Update your documentation with the new steps.

5. Communicate the changes and retrain others. This is important because you don't want others to continue doing it wrong if you've updated the procedure.

Making Systems Work for You

The keys to making systems work for you include tailoring them to your unique styles: organization style, communication style, and work style. If other people use your systems, you should also keep in mind their styles, and identify the best approach for everyone involved. This can take some trial and error, or an executive decision sometimes.

Resource Alert: To learn more about your organization, communication, and work styles, visit **ProceduresPro.com**.

Another key is document your systems so others can use them. This isn't a time to be territorial. Every single one of us needs a backup plan. And systems create a safety net we cannot afford to go without.

Once your documentation is created, remain flexible to updating and changing your systems as needed. Nothing should stay static. When you go into this knowing you need to remain flexible and open to new and better ways of doing things, it makes it easier to adapt to changes as they come.

Dealing With Change: People, Systems, and Processes

Once you create and test your systems and procedures, and you know they work, you must use them religiously for them to be most effective.

However, you also have to be open to modifying your procedures when situations change, responsibilities shift, or you find yourself facing a new organizational challenge. Perhaps you just got promoted and you have new responsibilities. This may require learning how to manage larger projects with more complexity.

If your company goes through a merger or acquisition, entire culture shifts can occur that force you to work differently.

Similarly, if you go through a significant personal transition – such as moving, having a baby, taking on a caregiver role, or switching from full- to part-time – it can shift your priorities and the way you work going forward.

These types of situations require a careful review of your procedures to identify what you need to adjust to ensure continued success in staying organized for the long haul.

Training Others to Use Your Procedures

While your procedures binder is an important resource for your job, to maximize its use, it's essential that you share it with your executive and those who may need to fill in for you. The following are a few tips to help you do just that:

- Inform your executive and people who fill in for you where your binder is located. Just because you know where it lives, doesn't mean everyone else does!

- Give those who cover for you a chance to go through it before your next scheduled time off.

- Answer any questions for those who fill in for you and make any necessary edits or additions if there are parts of your procedures that are confusing or incomplete.

- Make sharing your procedures binder part of your weekly or monthly one-on-one meetings with your executive. This provides built-in accountability to keep adding to it until it's complete!

- Use it before and/or during your annual performance review time. This is a major accomplishment, so make sure it gets noted on your review documentation.

It may take a little time for everyone to get used to having something to refer to while you're away. Just keep reminding them that the tool is there for their use.

Some people may be more open and willing to use it than others, and that's OK.

However, if there are snags in how tasks are completed while you're out – and you had your procedures documented, but they weren't used – make sure you politely note that with your manager.

Become a Procedures Pro!

When you begin the process of documenting your systems and procedures, it can seem like a daunting proposition. The key is to tackle your systems one by one, and never work on more than five procedures at a time as you do – ideally targeting one procedure per day. With an average of 22 workdays each month, next month at this time, you'll have 22 more documented procedures than you do now. The key is getting started!

When you take the simple step-by-step approach outlined in this book, and use the templates provided, you will put your office systems and procedures documentation on the fast track before you know it.

Don't delay another day! Get started on your administrative procedures binder right now. It's a fantastic resource for your daily use. And the next time someone needs to fill in for you while you're out of the office, you'll look smart because office operations won't come to a halt. You'll enjoy your time away more – with less stress. And you'll become known as the office procedures pro!

Success Story: "I had never fully appreciated the importance of having a procedure handbook until I received a sad call from my mother about the passing of my grandmother. It was shocking and confusing. I handed over (my procedures) to the relief admin very efficiently before heading to the burial to pay my last respects. My handbook included a brief introduction to the team, ongoing projects, upcoming meetings, file lists, working committees, and emergency contacts, among others. The admin who stood in for me was able to manage the office smoothly without interruptions."

– Florence Katono, Principal Administrative Assistant, Bank of Uganda

Appendix

APPENDIX A: COMPLETE CHECKLIST FOR SYSTEMS AND PROCEDURES DEVELOPMENT

 File Download: Visit **ProceduresPro.com** to download the following plans of action to get you started creating your office systems and documenting your administrative procedures.

My Systems Development Plan of Action

- ☐ Identify where you need to **create or improve an administrative system**.

- ☐ **Brainstorm what the ideal system** for that item would look like.

- ☐ **Test it**. Fine-tune it. Create your procedures related to it.

- ☐ **Implement your system(s)**.

- ☐ **Repeat**.

My Procedures Development Plan of Action

Step 1: Assemble the Right Tools for the Job.

- ☐ **Assemble the tools needed:**
    - ❏ **1 Extra Wide 3-Ring Binder**
    - ❏ **Tabbed Dividers – 8-Tab Sets** (2 sets)
    - ❏ **Sheet Protectors** (15-20)

☐ **Create a Binder Cover and Spine.**

☐ **Create a general Table of Contents.**

☐ **Create a permanent home** for your Admin Binder on your desk within arm's reach of where you primarily sit/work.

Step 2: Start Tracking Your Tasks for a Few Days.

☐ **Download and/or print the "Administrative Job Duties" tracking form at AllThingsAdmin.com** (or place it electronically on your PC desktop) to begin tracking your daily, weekly, monthly, annual tasks for both yourself and those you support.

☐ **Print 30 double-sided, 3-hole punched, BLANK procedures forms** to start handwriting your daily procedures on. Place them in a brightly colored file folder, which is easily accessible from where you sit at your desk.

Step 3: Pick Your Top Five Procedures. Repeat.

☐ Identify the first FIVE procedures you are going to document next week when you return to the office.

☐ _____

☐ _____

☐ _____

☐ _____

☐ _____

Procedures Ideas to Get You Started:

❏ Start the Day / End of the Day Checklists

❏ How to Make the Coffee

❏ Executives Regular Recurring Meetings

❏ How to Forward / Un-Forward Phones

❏ How to Check Voice Mail

Step 4: Identify What Else to Include.

☐ Check with ALL internal departments to see if they have procedures already documented that you can use:

❏ **Accounting** (expense reports, check requests, etc.)

❏ **Facilities** (how to get new keys, parking permits, maintenance requests, etc.)

❏ **Human Resources** (new hire checklists, termination checklists, employee handbook, etc.)

❏ **I.T.** (user guides for phones, voice mail, video conferencing equipment, conference bridge lines, etc.)

❏ **Mail Room** (internal mail procedures, USPS procedures, FedEx or UPS account and shipping info, etc.)

❏ **Marketing** (corporate logo use guidelines, business card ordering, etc.)

❏ **Travel** (online booking tool procedures, after hours info, etc.)

❏ _____

❏ _____

Procedures Ideas to Get You Started:

❏ Sorting/distributing the incoming mail and shipping packages – UPS/FedEx/USPS

❏ Office Supply Ordering

❏ New Employee Checklists

❏ Travel Itinerary and Travel Planning Details

❏ Event Planning Checklists

❏ Meeting and Agenda Prep Checklists

Brainstorm about procedures you should create for these general categories:

❏ **Basic Office Operations**

❏ _____

❏ _____

❏ _____

❏ _____

☐ **Information You Refer to Regularly**

    ☐ _____

    ☐ _____

    ☐ _____

    ☐ _____

☐ **Events / Meetings**

    ☐ _____

    ☐ _____

    ☐ _____

    ☐ _____

☐ **Technology You Use**

    ☐ _____

    ☐ _____

    ☐ _____

    ☐ _____

☐ **Department or Manager Specific Details**

    ☐ _____

    ☐ _____

    ☐ _____

    ☐ _____

🗀 **Checklists / Forms / Templates**

❒ _____

❒ _____

❒ _____

❒ _____

Step 5: Organize Your Binder for Ongoing Use.

🗀 **Finalize the tabbed sections** you need to include in your procedures binder.

🗀 **Update your table of contents** to reflect the order of the materials in your procedures binder.

🗀 **Add a recurring reminder to your calendar** or tasks to update this binder on at least a quarterly basis.

🗀 **Pat yourself on the back for all of the progress you've made on your administrative procedures project! Congratulations!**

Send Julie Perrine and her team an email sharing your awesome accomplishment! Email us at AdminSuccess@ AllThingsAdmin.com.

APPENDIX B: HOW TO USE THIS PROCEDURES BINDER WELCOME LETTER

☐ **Insert a "how to use this binder letter" at the beginning of the binder** for those filling in for you.

How to Use This Administrative Procedures Binder

If you're reading this right now, then you're probably filling in for me while I'm out of the office. Let me start by saying, "THANK YOU!"

Here's how you'll benefit the most from the information included in this procedures binder:

- Take a few minutes to familiarize yourself with the various tabbed sections of information included in this binder so you know what's here in case you need to refer to it.

- As you use the procedures outlined here, please make notes about anything that didn't make sense or could use additional clarification for future updates. This will help me make this tool even more useful in the future.

- If there were any procedures missing completely, please write them down and leave the list inside the front cover for me to review upon my return.

Thanks again for your assistance during my absence!

[Name]
[Title]
[Department]

OTHER BOOKS BY JULIE PERRINE

The Innovative Admin: Unleash the Power of Innovation In Your Administrative Career

Do you want to be the admin every executive wants by his or her side? Do you want to standout and have success in your career?

If your answer is "yes," then *The Innovative Admin* is for you!

This must-have book for admins helps you learn how to embrace innovative thinking that makes you invaluable to your executive, your co-workers, and your company. You will discover:

- What it means to be *The Innovative Admin.*

- How you can unleash your mind to think innovatively.

- Techniques you can use to bring out the administrative leader inside you.

- Ways you can tap into your creativity and initiative to get ahead.

The Innovative Admin empowers you to become the best you can be by enhancing your capacity for innovation!

TheInnovativeAdmin.com

The Organized Admin: Leverage Your Unique Organizing Style to Create Systems, Reduce Overwhelm, and Increase Productivity

Are you struggling to make sense of the disorganized chaos that is your workspace? Do you want more effective systems for keeping yourself and your executive organized? Do you want to better understand your unique organizing style?

The Organized Admin, offers advice, information, and resources on developing simple organizing systems that promote administrative career success. You will discover:

- What it means to be organized.

- How to organize everything from ideas and your workspace to meetings, travel, projects, and more!

- Insights into your unique organizing style preferences for time and space.

- Simple organizing principles you can implement in your day-to-day activities.

The Organized Admin empowers you to be a better administrative professional by teaching you simple, practical solutions for getting organized – and maintaining organization in all areas of your career!

TheOrganizedAdmin.com

OTHER PRODUCTS AND TRAINING FROM ALL THINGS ADMIN

AdminPro Training Series

AdminTech Crash Course

Administrative Procedures Toolkit

5 Days to Better Office Procedures Challenge

Kick-Start Creating Your Administrative Procedures Binder

Myers-Briggs Type Indicator Personality Assessments

Partnering With Your Executive

The Latest Innovation is You!

Professional Portfolio Builder

Creating a Powerful Professional Portfolio

Boost Your Professional Visibility With An Online Portfolio

Creating Your Strategic Administrative Career Plan

Travel Planning

Template Packages

Virtual Training On Demand

Visit **AllThingsAdmin.com** for information on these products and many more.

About the Author

Julie Perrine

Certified Administrative Professional® – Organizational Management
Certified Myers-Briggs Type Indicator® Administrator
Certified Productivity Pro® Consultant

Julie Perrine, CAP-OM, is an administrative expert, trainer, motivational speaker, and author. She is the founder and CEO of All Things Admin, a company dedicated to developing and providing innovative products, training, mentoring, and resources for administrative professionals.

Julie has more than 25 years of experience in the administrative profession spanning several industries and serving in corporate and startup settings. Her mission is to guide, encourage, and connect administrative professionals to the technologies, ideas, resources, and people they need to achieve professional success. Her upbeat, straightforward approach to handling opportunities and challenges gives admins proactive strategies for developing a plan, making progress, and achieving results.

Julie has created several innovative tools and programs for administrative professionals, including the Administrative Procedures Toolkit, Kick-Start Creating Your Administrative Procedures Binder Course, Professional Portfolio Builder, and ePortfolio Builder. She is the author of *The Innovative Admin: Unleash the Power of Innovation In Your Administrative Career, The Organized Admin: Leverage Your Unique Organizing Style to Create Systems, Reduce Overwhelm, and Increase Productivity*, and several eBooks – including *Your Career Edge: Create a Powerful Professional Portfolio,* and *Your Career Edge: Create a Professional Online Portfolio.*

Julie transformed a career as an administrative professional into several successful enterprises and shares her knowledge, expertise, and resources with individuals, corporations, and organizations as an online business model consultant, personality type strategist, and productivity expert.

Julie writes regularly for the Executive Secretary Magazine and All Things Admin, and her articles have been published in professional publications worldwide. She has been active in local and international organizations, including the International Association of Administrative Professionals and the National Association of Productivity and Organizing Professionals.

To inquire about having Julie Perrine speak at your next meeting, contact us at **AllThingsAdmin.com.**

Connect with All Things Admin

Website
AllThingsAdmin.com

Facebook
Facebook.com/AllThingsAdmin

Twitter
Twitter.com/JuliePerrine
Twitter.com/ProceduresPro

LinkedIn
LinkedIn.com/company/All-Things-Admin
LinkedIn.com/in/JuliePerrine

For downloadable resources mentioned in this book, visit ProceduresPro.com.

To inquire about having Julie Perrine speak at your next meeting, contact us through our website at **AllThingsAdmin.com.**

Acknowledgements

Writing my third book has been the most enjoyable author experience yet. Part of that is because procedures are my happy place. The other reason I attribute directly to creating a system for doing it with my second book that my team and I were able to follow and tweak as we worked on my third book. Systems work!

It is with gratitude and sincere appreciation that I thank the following people for their specific contributions:

- To my best friend and Chief Encouragement Officer – my husband, Todd.

- To my business coach, mentor, and friend – Maggie Jackson.

- To my A-team and their team members – Suzanne Bird-Harris, Amber Miller, Christine Morris, Ruth Pierce, Penny Sailer, and Michelle Witten.

- To my very patient and talented graphic designer – Chris George.

- To my outstanding illustrator – Sergey Myakishev.

- To my exceptional proofreaders and copy editors – Stephanie Berry and Kyle Woodley.

- To my fellow trainers, speakers, and colleagues – Lucy Brazier, Chrissy Scivicque, Peggy Vasquez, and Lisa Olsen – who have provided valuable expertise, insights, encouragement, support, and friendship throughout the writing process.

- To all of the administrative professionals worldwide who have participated in our procedures training courses and 5-Day Challenges and shared your challenges and successes with us as you created your procedures binders! Thank you for being part of the inspiration I need to continue creating training and resources to help you succeed.

END NOTES

1. Information Mapping, www.informationmapping.com, http://www.informationmapping.com/en/information-mapping/information-mapping/challenges.

2. FEMA, Protecting Your Business, www.fema.gov, June 24, 2016, https://www.fema.gov/protecting-your-businesses.

3. Nationwide, Most Small Business Owners at Risk for Disaster, www.nationwide.com, August 31, 2015, https://www.nationwide.com/about-us/083115-small-biz-survey.jsp.

4. Disaster Recovery Preparedness Benchmark, Disaster Recovery Preparedness Benchmark Survey, The State of Global Disaster Recovery Preparedness Annual Report 2014, www.drbenchmark.org, 2014, http://drbenchmark.org/wp-content/uploads/2014/02/ANNUAL_REPORT-DRPBenchmark_Survey_Results_2014_report.pdf.

5. Infrascale, 25 Data Disaster Recovery Statistics for 2015 (Infographic), www.infrascale.com, August 12, 2015, https://www.infrascale.com/25-disaster-recovery-statistics-for-2015-infographic/.

Index

Made in the USA
Coppell, TX
11 September 2020

37773765R00066

THE
ANTIQUES
GAME

THE ANTIQUES GAME

An insider's tips on
how to play it and win.

by David E. Hewett

Courtesy of *Maine Antique Digest*, Waldoboro, Me.

YANKEE, INC.
Dublin, New Hampshire

Designed and illustrated by Carl Kirkpatrick

Yankee, Inc., Dublin, New Hampshire 03444

First Edition

Copyright 1981, by Yankee, Inc.

Printed in the United States of America

Library of Congress Catalog Card No. 81-52196

ISBN: 0-911658-46-7

Table of Contents

ACKNOWLEDGMENTS

The people who help a writer see his book through from inception to completion are numerous. But I will mention only a few people here and hope that those not named will know my appreciation goes also to them. Thanks to Sam Pennington for his taking time out from the *Maine Antique Digest* to review the rough draft; Sandy Taylor at Yankee Books for the suggestions, editing, and polishing; and my wife, Janna, for typing, editing, cajoling, and believing. One other person cannot be left out. She believed and understood. Thanks, Mom.

Author's Preface

NEVER before have so many people been as conscious of the antiques business as they are today. Headlines scream at us daily from the front pages of our newspapers, "New Auction Record Set," "Record Price for a Piece of American Furniture." We hear about record prices on the network television news. We see the articles on American folk art in the weekly news magazines. We shake our heads in wonder at the little country auctions when a piece of wicker furniture brings $1750, as happened at a Vermont auction in 1980.

And it filters down. Small-shop owners report an upsurge in sales. People line up at appraisal booths at the antiques shows. But there is an undercurrent of worry among the professionals in the antiques business. We dealers used to sell primarily to knowledgeable collectors, but now we sell to investors and spur-of-the-moment buyers. The average person may not know what he is getting into when he invests in antiques, and if anything can kill the boom in antiques, that is it. As dealers, we want our customers to be informed, to know how the business works.

There are a lot of books on the market about antiques. Most of them are directed toward the person who already has a collecting interest. But by the time the novice collector gets around to reading such books, he may already have made some of the mistakes I would like now to correct.

I will tell you what antiques are, how to buy from a dealer, how and when to buy at auction, what antiques to invest in and when, when to avoid reproductions and when not to — in short, how this business I love works.

A word is in order about myself. I've been involved in all facets of the antiques business over the last eighteen years. I've worked for auctioneers; set up at shows; worked the flea markets; had a full-time, seven-days-a-week shop; repaired antiques; and been a "picker." There are a lot of words that are unique to the business of antiques, and "picker" is one of them. Pickers sell to dealers only. They haunt the auction halls, attend the shows, try to buy from private parties — all to get the merchandise they sell to dealers. They have to know antiques and be up to date on current trends and prices. Dealers would have a tough time existing without pickers, but then, dealers couldn't exist without you, the ultimate purchaser.

That's one of the reasons for this book. You are necessary to the antiques business. Those of us who make our living in the business want you to be happy. We want you to feel good about your purchases.

It never fails to amaze me how many people and steps are involved in the circuitous route that an antique might follow in its journey to a dealer's shop. The dealer could have bought a particular item from a private party or from a picker, or he might have purchased it at an auction. But where did the auctioneer get it? Did it come from yet another auction or from a yard sale? Or was it bought from a family home by that vanishing breed of character known as a door-knocker?

The days of door-knocking are pretty much over in New England now. There was a time when dealers would wander about the countryside looking for suitable houses to approach with the door-knocking patter of "any antiques for sale?"

Once they had a foot in the door, it was almost necessary to shoot them to get them out. I have heard this story about "John," a legendary dealer now deceased, from enough sources to think it might be true. He'd go to a home he'd already heard about as having two or three great items mixed in with the average household pieces.

As soon as someone answered the door, he'd go into a great rushing speech about how he was an antiques dealer terribly low on stock, and was willing to pay anything for pieces he could use. Before the surprised occupant could say anything, John would reach for the first piece in sight — be it porch rug, beat-up rocker, or even, in one case, the broom —

and offer an outrageous price for it. He'd offer $15 for the broom. Dollar signs would sparkle before the eyes of the lady of the house as John swept past. Out would come a note pad, and the game was begun.

"Hundred and fifty for that chair with the broken leg. Ninety-five for that cup and saucer. Don't worry about the coffee in it, my man will take care of it."

From room to room they would go. He in the lead, writing figures furiously on the pad, she trailing, with visions of new furniture, paying off the mortgage, maybe a new hairdo. After covering the house from cellar to attic, he'd rapidly calculate the figures. "That comes to eight thousand, five hundred, right?"

She, flabbergasted, would try to think. It's only the junk they've picked up over the years, some of it left to her. "All that money! Sure, sure, eight thousand, five hundred."

"OK. Now here's what I'm going to do, lady. As you see I've only got my car with me now. I'll have to get the big truck up here tomorrow morning. You get the stuff ready and my man will load it. I've got to hit the road, got another house to look at. Let's see, I'll just take a couple pieces that will fit in the car now. Maybe just those two crocks from the attic, and that one chair from the sitting room. Now where are they on this list? Oh, here they are. Two crocks, four dollars, chair, five dollars. That's nine, right?"

Whipping out a massive roll of bills, he'd pay her $9. "I'll pay for the rest when we load the truck. Have to check to make certain I got all I paid for, you know."

With his two crocks and one chair safely beside him, he would make a hasty departure, leaving her sitting there with visions of greenbacks dancing in her head. Of course he would never return. He hadn't even given his name, and if by some accident of fate she ever ran into him again, he'd explain, "I decided I didn't need the rest."

Eventually dealers of his ilk vanished. The word spread. Door-knockers found hard pickings in the country. People started reading price guides. They soon became aware of values. Other dishonest methods and people began to fill the void left by the door-knocker, however. There are fakers, liars, dishonest auctioneers, thieves, and cheats, and I'll describe them throughout this book. Some people would prefer to keep it all a secret, but the antiques industry has nothing to fear from informing the customer, for once you know how the business works, you will be able to spot these rip-off artists.

The good dealers, the honest auctioneers, want you to be aware of values. We don't enjoy it when, in our shops, you sneer at pieces that are marked at fair prices. We want you to pay a reasonable price for a piece at auction. Consignors will stop consigning if you won't pay fair prices.

As the values of antiques rise so does the number of fakes; reproductions; reconstructed, rebuilt, repaired, and otherwise-altered pieces being offered in the marketplace. But it isn't just the retail customer who faces the chance of owning a fake. Most dealers have bought at least one fake in their careers. We usually sell it to you.

Confession may be good for the soul but it's hell on the pocketbook. Sometimes a dealer will tell the customer if a piece isn't right, but quite often he will simply drop the offending article into an auction. You are on your own then. You need to know how to spot a fake, how to tell if parts have been replaced, how to know if a finish is original, and if a piece is still a good buy. I'll describe some of the telltale things to look for.

This past year I have sat at auctions and watched sober, intelligent adults (people who carefully check out the prices on the cereal boxes in the neighborhood supermarkets) consistently overbid at auctions. They have seen their savings-account interest fail to keep pace with rising inflation, and so, there they are, investing in antiques. Take, for example, the fellow who paid $750 for a repainted Boston rocker at auction. At $150 there were no dealers left bidding. But climb the price did, until that $750 figure was reached. We dealers looked at each other in wonder. There was no way that particular chair was worth that kind of money.

Don't misunderstand — dealers make mistakes. But too many mistakes and we are out of business. So, by and large we must and do understand prices.

Auction prices for the average or mediocre items have been consistently high and occasionally ridiculous this past year. I've watched a bidder pay over $900 for a Windsor chair with replaced legs. He never knew they were replaced until a reputable dealer pointed this out to him later. The buyer was very disappointed. He'd bought the chair as an investment, assuming it was all original and therefore a good buy. The price wasn't outrageous, but it was more than enough for a piece with repairs. As an investment it was a poor choice. No piece of furniture with major replacements will increase in value as much as a "straight," or all original, piece will.

Two other bidders ran the price on a highboy up to over $12,000. The consensus among the dealers who examined the highboy was that it was a "married" piece — that is, that the top and bottom sections of the tall chest of drawers on legs had come from two separate highboys. None of the interested dealers bid over $5000. If it was a married piece — and only close examination would reveal that — someone will be in for a surprise when that piece re-enters the auction arena.

An investment by definition is an outlay of money for income or profit. People have been investing in antiques for decades, and very nice profits have been made from these investments, but if you want to invest in antiques, be sure to do it sensibly.

There are some very simple rules to follow for wise investing. I'll tell you how to buy for investment, when to buy, and when not to. Some of us in the trade are worried about the present trend of buying indiscriminately. We see a time in the future when you might decide to unload your investments. We'd like to see you realize a profit and continue to buy from us.

We hear you at auctions. "Why did the auctioneer do that? Why were those dealers laughing at the person who bought those chairs? What does 'sold to the book' mean?" More of you are attending auctions than ever before. The procedure at an auction shouldn't be a mystery to you: I'll describe what you can expect at an auction and how the dishonest auctioneer operates.

Once you understand the business, once you know the rules, the antiques collecting or investing experience can be a very pleasurable one. The vast majority of dealers and auctioneers are hard-working, honest people. Most of us love what we do, enjoy meeting customers, making new friends, and furthering the love of antiques. We'd like you to trust us, to buy our wares, and to come back for more.

Courtesy of Robert W. Skinner, Inc., Bolton, Mass.

1

Early Furniture

MUCH of the merchandise found today either in the average dealer's shop or at an average country auction is not antique. To be recognized by the government as antique, an object must be at least one hundred years old. We have come to accept items a lot newer than that as "antiques." Sure, there are still a lot of shops that only deal in authentic antiques, and many of them have much earlier cut-off dates than one hundred years ago. Many of the better auction houses don't like the newer items, but if they wish to stay open year-round, they are forced into running the Victorian-era antiques, the Arts and Crafts Movement furniture of the early 1900s, stuff our parents knew as Mission Oak, and even later pieces.

We are already accepting as antiques many things that legally won't reach that status until well into the twenty-first century: the majority of wicker furniture, most brass beds, an awful lot of oak furniture, a variety of clocks. The list could go on and on. But for a real eye opener, get hold of a Sears Roebuck catalogue from the mid 1930s or even 1940 and see what our parents were offered. Surprising, isn't it, that so many items found today in the average antiques shop or among the auction offerings were being sold by Sears just forty to fifty years ago.

I'm going to stay with the rule that an "antique" must be at least one hundred years old. Younger than that and it's old but not antique. A lot of pieces are almost antique. Victorian furniture is difficult to categorize since many styles of Victorian-era furniture were sold long after the cut-off date. You probably refer to these pieces as antiques if you own them. Fine, so will I. But when I write of a piece as a true antique, it means it's over one hundred years old.

The first antique most people buy is usually a piece of furniture. When I ran a full-time, open (as opposed to "closed," meaning selling to dealers only) shop, furniture was the one item that sold to non-collectors consistently. People who knew absolutely nothing about Chippendale or Hepplewhite would stop in to look around for a good, usable antique chair or table or bureau. These items are the bread-and-butter of the antiques business.

Furniture does have certain styles and periods, and a buyer is well advised to understand them. A piece that was made during the time span in which that particular style flourished is said to be a "period" piece. (A true period piece commands the top dollar value for that item.) A piece with a "style" could have been produced any time since the style evolved. That's an important distinction. New furniture in a factory showroom can be accurately described as being such-and-such a style. Don't be misled.

Before you start buying any early furniture — whether for investment or for your personal collection — you should know about fakes, reproductions, restorations, and replacements (see Chapter 5). All furniture suffers a degree of wear over the years, some much more than others. Here in New England there are some very fine craftspeople repairing and rebuilding furniture. I know people who delight in rebuilding damaged pieces of early furniture.

This isn't a new phenomenon. I've seen a rebuilding job that had to have been done at least fifty years ago that stretched a Queen Anne side-chair into a lovely little love seat. I bought in Maine several years ago a country Chippendale lamp table that was built out of two chairs. It was a good old job. Just keep in mind that there are people around who are capable of these things, and you should be on the lookout if you're searching for something authentic.

Also remember that one component that you can identify and place in a specific period doesn't make a piece a period piece. A few years ago I joined the mad rush of area dealers who were driving several dusty miles on dirt back roads early in the morning to a well-advertised yard sale featuring "period

18

Chippendale furniture." We were a forlorn group, standing there around the mahogany table and chairs and watching the proud owner putting price tags with multi-thousand dollar figures on his 1930s-era offerings.

"Yes," I agreed, "that is a ball-and-claw foot. Yes, that is a cabriole leg. Uh-huh, that's mahogany all right. Right, there are carved shells on the front rails. But — I really don't think they are period." He was adamant, and even hauled some furniture books out of the house to point out the similar details. We, in turn, showed him the factory-smooth undersides of the chairs, the obvious fifty-year-old screws; we told him about the lack of hand-done detail and that there was no evidence of two hundred years' worth of wear. But it was all in vain. He went back to those ball-and-claw feet as proof.

A piece of furniture is only as old as its latest stylistic component or original-construction detail. It's not unusual to hear an auctioneer describe the Hepplewhite "type" or "style" legs on a lamp stand to a bemused crowd. It's not unusual either to see two novice collectors get carried away with the description and bid up to a period price on a 1920s-era piece of furniture.

Let's look at the styles of furniture made in America starting from the earliest. I can hear you now: "Wait a minute, I just want to buy some antiques, I don't want to learn a lot of names and dates." OK. But what I'm going to give you are the most important styles and the name of one of the most important cabinetmakers in America. Period Pilgrim Century, William and Mary, Queen Anne, Chippendale, important examples of Hepplewhite and Sheraton furniture, and original pieces made by Duncan Phyfe are what are known as "big bucks" pieces. Chippendale furniture at this writing holds the record for the highest auction price paid for a piece of American furniture: $360,000 (plus a ten percent buyer's commission) for a three-drawer chest.

You may not be able to invest that amount of money but you're going to have to pay heavily for any decent piece of period furniture. If you don't know styles, can't tell old from fake, Heaven help you.

To make it a little easier, here's a chart of approximate style dates:

Pilgrim Century	before 1700
William and Mary	1700-1720
Queen Anne	1720-1755
Chippendale	1755-1790
Hepplewhite	1785-1810
Sheraton	1795-1820
Duncan Phyfe	1807-1820 (active long after this date producing American Empire)

Be aware that the first furniture in America was brought here from other countries and huge quantities have been brought here since. I'm dealing only with furniture *produced* in America. The best market in the world for American furniture is America.

Early styles of furniture made in America are as follows. (See illustrations at the end of this chapter.)

Pilgrim Century: We use this broad name for almost all furniture made in America before 1700. The style of Pilgrim Century furniture resembles the furniture of the country the Pilgrims came from, England. The wood used was most often oak, although pine, maple, hickory, ash, and beech made appearances. Most (some collectors would say nearly all) Pilgrim Century furniture has been collected and is now in museums. Visit them to see the great Bible boxes, low chests, chests on ball feet, court cupboards, butterfly and communion tables, cradles, and Brewster, Carver, and wainscot chairs. In the highly unlikely event you are offered a Pilgrim Century piece of furniture, be extremely wary. Compare it to all the known museum examples and then still doubt. There are a few good dealers selling Pilgrim Century furniture but don't expect pieces to show up at an average auction. It would take microscopic examination of the wood to confirm a piece is American and experts even question some of those results.

William and Mary: This furniture began to be made in America about 1700 and continued until 1720. Walnut, or maple with walnut veneer, was the most common wood used, although pine was used as a secondary wood for the components that are out of sight, such as drawer runners and glue blocks. The style was that of the rich English furniture in vogue at that time. Chairs were often caned and began to feature carved scrolls and "Spanish feet," or trifid feet (with three toe-like projections). Chests were raised to sit on a frame featuring inverted bowl turnings. The hardware on drawers was often brass drop pulls. Day beds (backless couches with one end resembling a chair) made their appearance and took on Flemish details. William and Mary furniture is about as rare as Pilgrim Century, although occasionally a chair, highboy, or chest will emerge from a private collection.

Queen Anne: In 1720 the style known as Queen Anne started to spread. By the end of the period, in 1755, this style was being copied and used in all of the furniture-making centers. We are able to spot certain characteristics and name conclusively the area in which the furniture was made since the woods used varied with the woods locally available. Legs on furniture were curved, and called cabriole. The form of a piece was often undulating. Legs terminated in pad or cushioned-pad feet, and sometimes the Spanish foot was used. In the Philadelphia area, ball-and-claw feet made their first appearance and are rare today. Highboys lost the stretcher construction supporting the legs. The undulating form and cabriole legs are the most easily identifiable marks of Queen Anne furniture. This style does show up in the shops and at auction; however, good examples are scarce and therefore very expensive.

Chippendale: The next great period of American furniture took the name of Thomas Chippendale, an English cabinetmaker who published his design book in 1754. The furniture makers must have been hungry for a change because his designs first swept England, then America. His designs featured one rococo detail — the shell — that identifies them as Chippendale, although transitional Queen Anne furniture is sometimes found with carved shells. The ball-and-claw foot came into universal use though Chippendale never showed it in his design book. Hairy, pawed feet and straight-legged, straight-blocked feet were also used. The backs of chairs featured undulating bow-shaped tops and carved and pierced splats. We find some of the larger case pieces of furniture constructed with blocked fronts. Serpentine shapes also were employed. Tables were often built with straight legs (usually fluted), and usually with scrolled or pierced brackets. Highboys were topped off with pediments. The more ornate pieces were highly carved on the knees of the legs or along the bases or skirts. Mahogany was used most frequently, exclusively by some cabinetmakers. The Chippendale style flourished from 1755 until 1790.

Federal: Federal furniture actually encompasses two consecutive styles. The Federal period runs from 1780 until 1820. As applied to furniture, it's a relatively new term. Thirty years ago we were still identifying the period by the names of two cabinetmakers, George Hepplewhite and Thomas Sheraton. Hepplewhite's designs are the earliest, running from 1785 to 1810. Hepplewhite furniture features a feeling of delicacy. Legs are square — never cabriole or fluted — and taper to the bottom. Chair backs are oval or shield shaped. The larger pieces of furniture were often inlaid or veneered, sometimes in very intricate patterns. String inlays, or "bands," were used to outline the various parts of a piece.

By 1810 Sheraton's designs began to replace Hepplewhite's. Sheraton furniture has legs that are round and reeded; chair backs are rectangular. Often we find ornamentation of carving, painting, or brass. The chairs known as Sheraton evolved into early thumb-back designs with rush seats. Identify Sheraton by the round, turned legs.

Under the heading of Federal furniture one has to include the products of the New York cabinetmaker Duncan Phyfe. Although after 1820 his work followed the style known as American Empire (see Chapter 2), the pieces he produced before that date took the Sheraton style and pushed it to its limits. His best pieces are reeded, acanthus-leaf carved, fitted with ornamental brass hardware, and made from the best grades of mahogany. Indeed, mahogany remained the favorite wood of cabinetmakers through the whole Federal period. Phyfe introduced Grecian details to this country. His designs were sometimes unorthodox and deviated widely from Sheraton, but they are Federal and very desirable.

Bear in mind that Chippendale, Hepplewhite, and Sheraton were all cabinetmakers who published books of design for fellow cabinetmakers. Therefore, we speak of a piece of furniture as being of the Sheraton or Chippendale style. Some of their styles were being produced in the countryside long after they went out of fashion in the cities. It is also possible to find pieces made by craftsmen who blended two or more major styles into one piece of furniture.

This entire era following the Revolution was one of exciting design developments. Craftsmen borrowed freely from each other's ideas. Regional differences became more apparent. If mahogany wasn't available, pine was used instead. Perhaps a craftsman would decide he didn't like an urn inlay on the front of his sideboard even though the pattern book showed one; well, he'd carve a pine tree there instead.

I can't underscore enough the importance of the fact that for a piece of furniture to be called period, it must have been *made* in the period during which the style was prevalent. I sat at a country auction once and watched an auctioneer sell a 1920s bow-front Sheraton-style chest to an excited bidder for over $700. She turned to her husband and asked, "Isn't that a great buy for a genuine antique?" He nodded affirmatively.

The rest of us, the dealers near her, just smiled. We'd bid on it too, up to $200. We were interested because it was a good copy done in Sheraton style. It was a usable chest, but it definitely was not an antique.

Someday she (or her heirs) might try to sell it. Someone is going to have to tell her it isn't a period piece.

Determining the age of a piece of old furniture involves a variety of factors. You first have to match it to a style. For example, does the piece have the cabriole legs of either the Queen Anne or Chippendale period? If so, that would date it between 1720 and 1790. How about the feet? Ball and claw? Probably Chippendale. Is there anything on the piece that suggests a later style? A piece of furniture can be dated by its *latest* stylistic feature. William and Mary furniture doesn't have Chippendale pediments. Chippendale furniture doesn't have Sheraton reeded legs.

Here are guidelines I use to determine how old a piece is:

1. What style is it? What are the years for that style?
2. Does it match other known examples of the style?
3. Are the woods used in this piece consistent with woods known to be used during this era?
4. Is it built like other examples from the era?
5. Are the tool marks on the piece consistent with those made by tools used in the era?
6. Are the screws, nails, hardware used on the piece consistent with its apparent age?

I'm not concerned with repairs or replacements yet; I'm trying to date the basic piece. Remember, telling how old a piece of furniture is involves a juggling act between two factors: **1.** In what era does the style place the piece, and; **2.** What date do the construction and material suggest? A piece of furniture with Chippendale styling suggests a date of before 1790. If there are modern circular-saw marks on the drawer sides, if there is no trace of the early tool marks that one would expect on a piece of early furniture, and if there is a plywood drawer bottom, the piece was probably made much later or has had such extensive restoration, and poorly done restoration at that, so as to lower its value drastically. The questions above should be asked about any furniture, whether it be an American Empire piece with its clunky lines, scrolled feet, and often veneered finishes, or a buttermilk-painted country pine piece.

Let me leave you with some advice about investing in

early furniture: if you can afford to buy anything you desire, if you don't mind overpaying for a piece, if you don't mind the sarcastic asides and withering glances you receive from the dealers at an auction when you pay twice as much as a piece is worth, then ignore all that I've written. This book is not for you. But if you want to realize a profit on your investment, if you enjoy the feeling of knowing that the Hepplewhite lamp stand that sits proudly beside the new sofa is a true period piece, then you have to take the time to study antiques. Read the books I've listed at the end of Chapter 2. Visit the museums. Talk to the dealers. It is definitely worth the time and effort.

Fig. 1

Fig. 3

Fig. 2

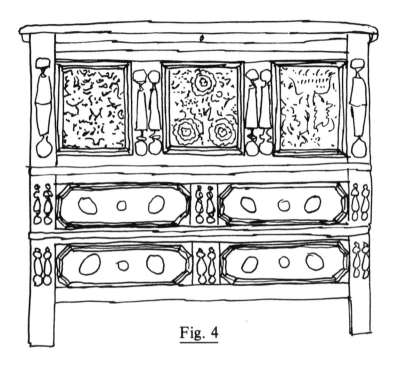

Fig. 4

PILGRIM CENTURY

---

1. Child's chair, possibly of Massachusetts origin. Like all really early pieces, expect missing or replaced parts. Almost no child's chair exists today with the original foot rest. Don't believe it if someone tells you a Pilgrim Century chair has its original rush seat. Three hundred years is just too long for it to have survived. 2. Tavern table of pine with maple legs and turnings. Note the thickness of the legs and stretchers. The drop finial is often missing. 3. Ball-and-sausage turned chair of a type found in the New Jersey area. European counterparts do exist, however. Provenance is critical. 4. Tulip and sunflower paneled chest from Connecticut River Valley, most often found with replaced raised decorations. Sometimes the lid or bottoms of the legs will have been replaced. Rarely found with any original paint.

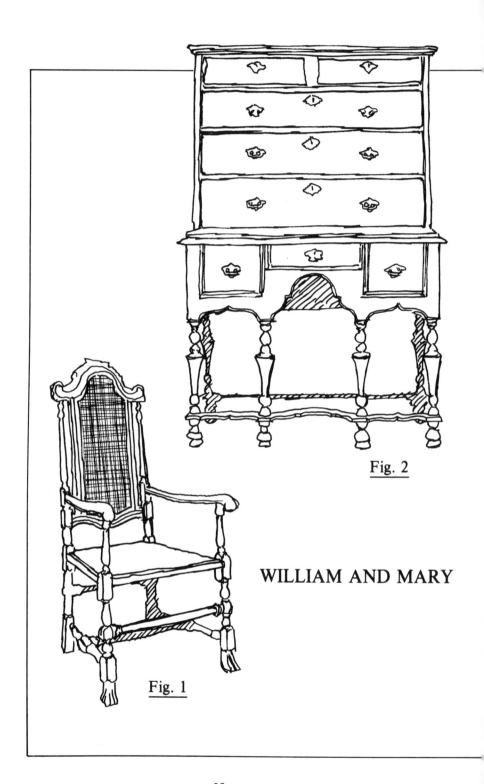

Fig. 2

WILLIAM AND MARY

Fig. 1

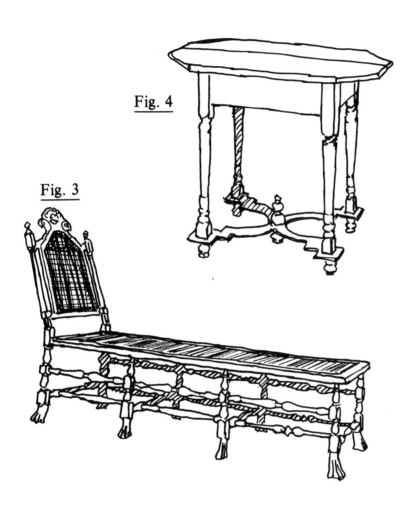

Fig. 4

Fig. 3

1. New York armchair with Spanish feet and caned back. If you ever find one with the original caning, don't replace it even if it is damaged. Original cane is rare, hence valuable. 2. Walnut New England highboy with trumpet-shaped turnings on the legs. The flat stretchers echo the cut-out shape of the base. Often found with replaced legs and stretchers. 3. Day bed with Spanish feet and caned back. 4. Octagonal-top pine tavern table. The flat cross stretcher has a fifth foot under it for support. Early tables like this one frequently have lost the original foot or finial and have replacements.

29

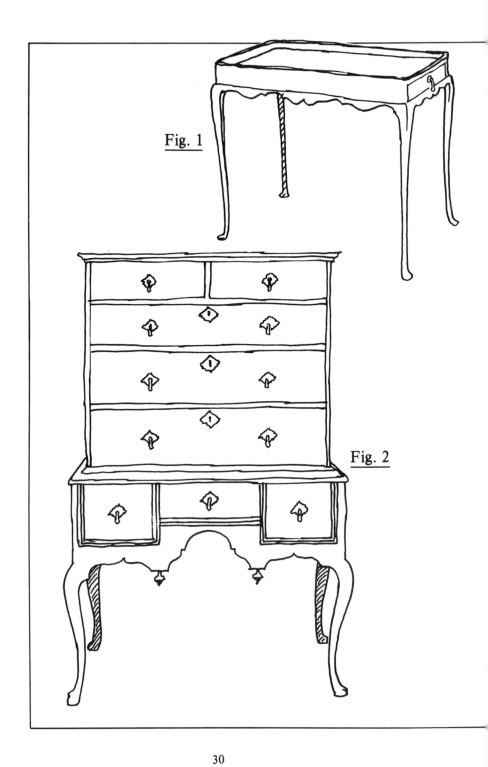

Fig. 1

Fig. 2

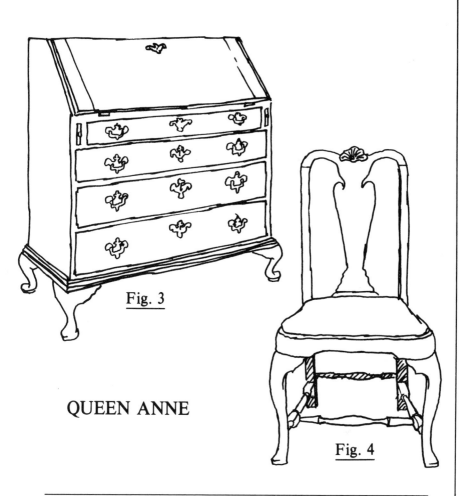

Fig. 3

QUEEN ANNE

Fig. 4

1. Mahogany New England tea table with end drawer. Finding a piece like this with the original tear-drop pull and unrepaired legs would be a rarity. 2. Small highboy from Massachusetts. Pieces of this size (just over five feet) are rarer than the larger examples. Note the distinctive Queen Anne brass drop pulls. 3. Fall-lid desk with cabriole legs and pad feet, also called bandy legs. 4. Walnut sidechair with shell carving on the crest rail and graceful leg stretchers.

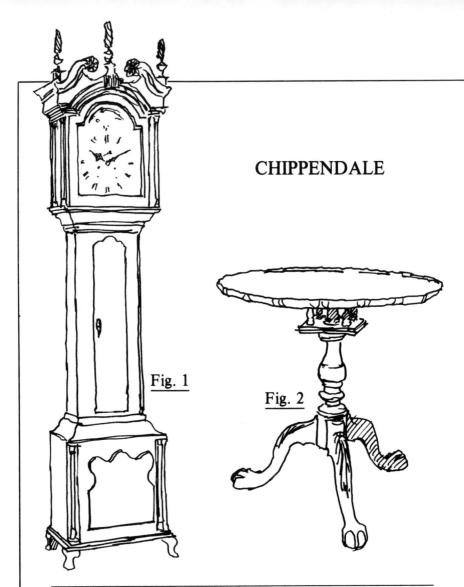

Fig. 1

Fig. 2

1. Tall clock from Philadelphia with graceful carved finials and broken arch pediment. Early tall clocks have often suffered damage from careless handling or moving. Examine the parts on the bonnet for replacement or repair. 2. Mahogany tea table with a ''pie-crust'' top. The whole top revolves on the base because of the birdcage structure underneath. Note the carving on the knees of the legs, and the ball-and-claw feet. 3. Walnut armchair that clearly exhibits Chippendale styling: pierced carved splat, shell motif, acanthus-leaf carving on the knees, and ball-and-claw feet. 4. Mahogany block-front chest of drawers. Note how the shape of the top, the drawer fronts, and the base molding follow the same contour.

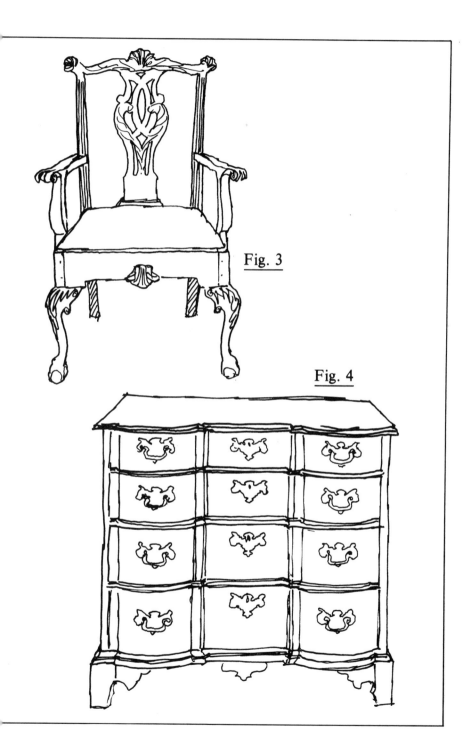

Fig. 3

Fig. 4

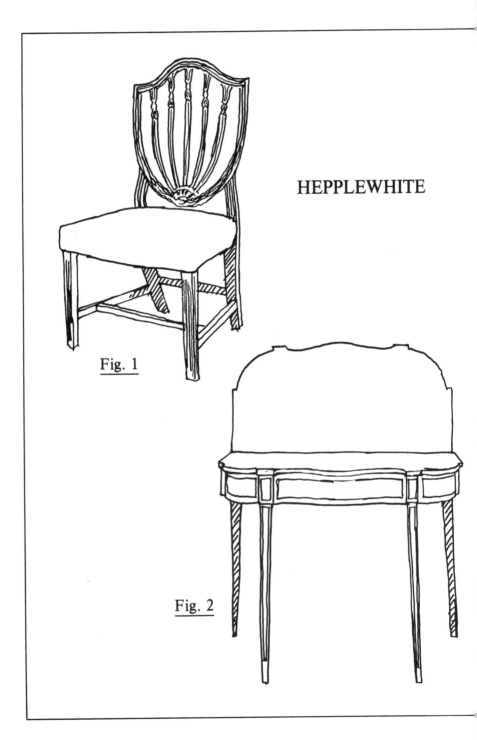

HEPPLEWHITE

Fig. 1

Fig. 2

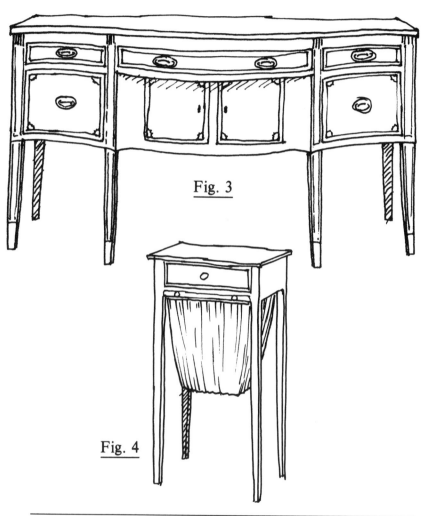

Fig. 3

Fig. 4

1. Mahogany sidechair from Philadelphia. Usually made in sets, and much more valuable as such. If you own a set, keep it that way — don't sell just one chair. 2. Massachusetts card table in mahogany, with various inlays. 3. Graceful mahogany sideboard from New York State with inlaid fan design. These pieces are sometimes over six feet long. 4. Sewing or work table, valuable with the original paint and rarely found with original sewing or scrap bag.

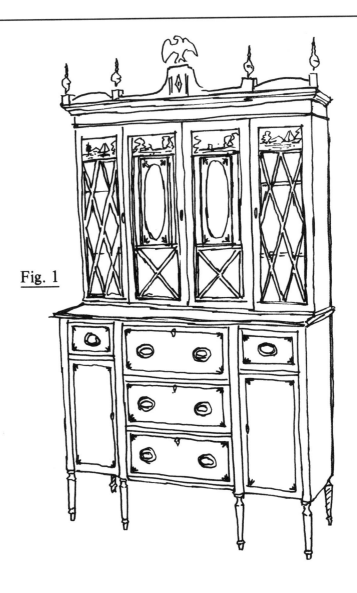

Fig. 1

1. Mahogany breakfront secretary-bookcase from Massachusetts. It is rare to find one with the original painted glass panels and brass finials intact. 2. Mahogany sofa from Connecticut. Note the spiral reeded legs. 3. Massachusetts "lolling" or "Martha Washington" type armchair with reeded legs. 4. Delicate mahogany work table from Boston, with various inlays.

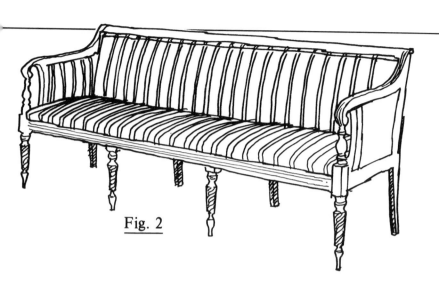

Fig. 2

SHERATON

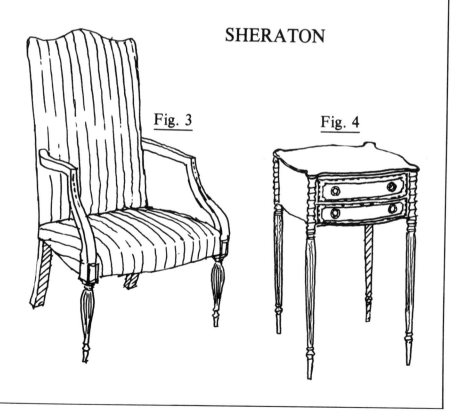

Fig. 3

Fig. 4

37

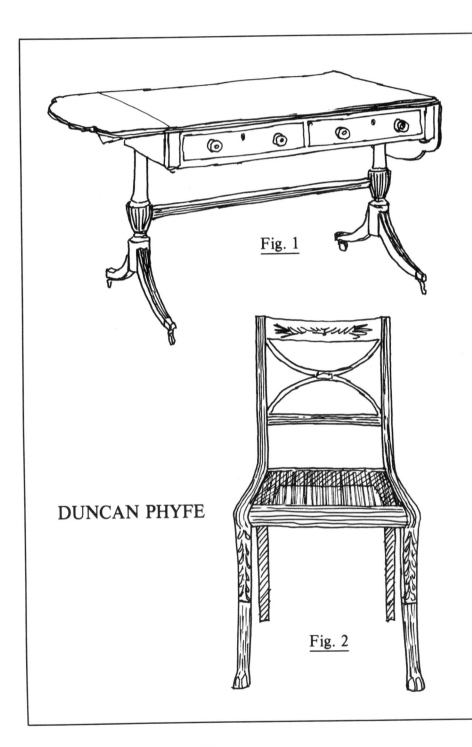

Fig. 1

DUNCAN PHYFE

Fig. 2

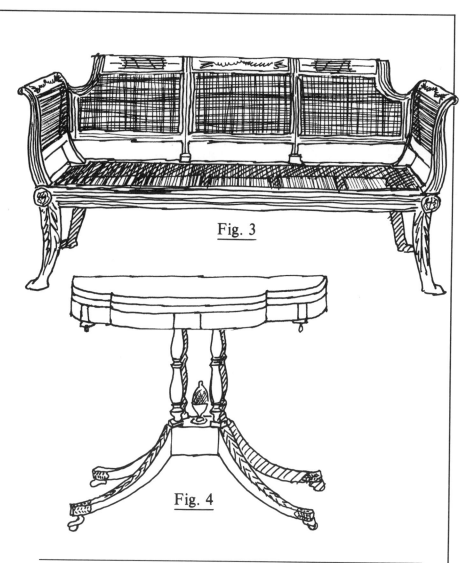

Fig. 3

Fig. 4

1. Mahogany sofa table with drawers on both sides. Note the reeded decoration. The better furniture companies have been reproducing designs like this for years. Look for early construction techniques, signs of wear, and early castors and pulls. 2. and 3. Chair and settee, made and carved during Phyfe's best period (1815-20), showing crisp, detailed carving on the crest rails, paw feet, and reeded decoration. 4. Mahogany card table with carved pineapple finial and brass castors.

Courtesy of *Maine Antique Digest*, Waldoboro, Me.

2

Furniture Made After 1820

THE majority of furniture available for sale today was made after 1820. Starting with those pieces made during what is known as the American Empire period (1820 to 1850) and extending all the way up to the products of the Arts and Crafts period of 1880 to 1920, this furniture encompasses many different types, styles, and finishes, and has its own individual collecting fraternity.

Americans produced an enormous amount of products during the nineteenth century. We imported a great deal, too. The fact that so much has survived into the 1980s suggests that many people have an affection for the past. But beyond the simple accumulation of yesterday's artifacts in the attic, there did exist early collectors — people who sought out examples of lost practices and disused items. It wasn't until the latter part of the nineteenth century, however, that the distinction of being an antiques collector began to have much honor.

Today's collectors can exhibit with pride their Federal living rooms or their groupings of antique hooked rugs. There is no stigma attached to the fact that the pieces were previously owned by someone else. Our ancestors were not as fortunate in their situations.

Friends of mine in New York City tell of how they started their Renaissance Revival collection of Victorian furniture only a few years ago. In walnut and burl, this furniture was popular between 1850 and 1870. Much of it was produced in Grand Rapids, Michigan.

While driving through a neighborhood near Brooklyn

one morning, they saw chairs piled up by the curb awaiting the garbage truck's arrival. They stopped and asked the owners if they could have them. Conversation disclosed that there was a lot more of the "stuff" if they wanted it.

After a few purchases at very low prices, they were introduced to neighbors who had more pieces. Within a week they had completely furnished their dining and living rooms with very desirable Victorian furniture. Driving by shortly after, they saw a new chrome-and-plastic dining room set being proudly unloaded. It was a classic case of upward mobility.

One thing to remember about all categories of furniture is that America was a very industrial country right from the beginning. Even some of the most sought-after early furniture was produced in a factory-like manner. One man sawed the lumber, another glued the boards, someone else did the carving, and another put on the finish. Don't get too carried away when an auctioneer tries to tell you that a piece is "hand made." We still use our hands.

What *is* important to remember is that the more highly carved, elaborate, veneered pieces were usually produced by the city cabinetmakers and furniture factories. Country craftsmen copied these pieces and usually simplified the details. So we find the dark varnished American Empire furniture with veneered cases of mahogany, walnut, or tiger maple with vigorous, impressive lines being produced in the cities. But the country pieces, made of softwood and with a painted finish, sometimes exhibit a true gracefulness of line.

American Empire furniture poses a real dilemma for antiques dealers. We have watched it being sold at auction for years and it has never realized high prices. I recently saw an American Empire sideboard-server in tigered veneer bring only $170. Dealers feel that customers still won't accept American Empire styling. But the furniture is well made. Actually, that's an understatement; it's *excellently* made. There has been little furniture made in America since that is built as well. Most of the veneering I've examined shows the work of craftsmen who excelled at their work. Joints are solid, drawers

42

are excellently built. Most pieces of this style are finished in dark-colored varnishes that are quite easy to strip.

A dealer friend in New Hampshire describes his experience with this furniture. "For forty years, I've heard people talk about how American Empire furniture is going to take off next year. If I put away all the damn Empire I've been offered, this whole barn would be stuffed." He waves an expressive arm at a monster of a barn. "And do you know what? I'd still be waiting for it to take off."

He's right. American Empire furniture commanded better prices in the 1920s and '30s than it brought in the '70s. A damaged piece of it only has one thing going for it in New England: some of us buy it for the parts. We sell parts to those very clever craftspeople who use the pieces in their rebuilding or reconstructing projects.

I've seen the two small top drawers from an American Empire chest stripped of their veneer, refinished to natural pine, and made into silverware drawers for a pine step-back cupboard. The cupboard brought an extra $500 from an auction-goer because of the drawers. The piece became a near fake.

I don't know of any style of furniture that is as under-priced in America as American Empire. You have to examine the pieces carefully. Some of the more clunky styles won't sell much better in five years than they do now, but to ignore a whole style because of the crudity of a few pieces is a mistake.

Any furniture that is comparable in price to the poorly made examples showing up today in the new-furniture show-rooms is a good buy providing you can use it. Forget all the rules about telling if a piece is original or not, period or repro-duction — if you like a piece and can use it in your home, and if it is priced competitively with new furniture, buy it. The new stuff will wear out; so will the old — but if you like it, buy it.

Antiques dealers have their prejudices, so when you've just paid $350 for an American Empire secretary at a country auction and the crowd at the back of the room begins to mut-ter, "No piece of Empire is worth that!" or "A fool and his money are soon parted," just smile and ask, "Have you priced a secretary made out of plywood, masonite, and staples at a new-furniture showroom lately?''

From about 1850 on, the factories really began to turn out the furniture, and ran through all sorts of revivals: Gothic Revival, Rococo Revival, Egyptian Revival, Japanese Revival, Louis XVI Revival, Renaissance Revival, Elizabethan Revival. Designers couldn't seem to do anything but copy a style that had already existed. Large quantities of this furniture have survived. Good examples of Victorian furniture have been trucked out of New England for the last decade, first going to the nearby cities, next to the Deep South, finally making the trek to the West. Last year I was offered a job driving truckloads of furniture to Alaska.

Victorian furniture is found in strange places. While visiting the Shelburne Museum in Shelburne, Vermont, a few years ago, a friend of mine and I decided to get out of the motel habit that so many dealers are prone to. We checked the newspapers and decided to stay at a house that advertised accommodations for overnight guests.

Situated on the shore of Lake Champlain, the large ark of a place we chose was built around the 1870s. Two elderly sisters welcomed us. The inside of the house was as much a museum in its own way as anything the Shelburne could offer. The rooms downstairs were full to bursting with black horsehair-covered sofas, marble-topped tables, and elaborately scrolled, tall hat racks.

Our room was a showplace of Japanese Revival furniture. The dresser was a full seven feet tall and the headboard of the bed matched it. Washstands, side chairs, commodes, and occasional stands competed for space.

When the ladies mentioned their rate of $7 a night, I asked them if they'd ever thought of selling any of their treasures. "Oh no, dear me, these pieces were Mother's and Father's. They go with the house. We couldn't take them away from it.'' I didn't ask again.

Talking prices to people who don't want to sell is a futile exercise, but I've wondered since if they were aware of the thousands they were sitting on while taking in overnight guests at $7 a night.

The very best pieces of Victorian furniture will now bring several thousand dollars. In 1980 an ornately carved table made in the 1850s by the New York City cabinetmaker John Henry Belter sold for $60,000. If your grandfolks' house is furnished with quality Victorian furniture, it would be a good idea to talk them into calling in a competent appraiser.

The rules for telling whether a piece is original apply to Victorian furniture, too. Know how it was made, know the styles, examine the finish. The newer a piece of furniture is, the more original the finish should be. It's easier to make repairs on a newer piece than on an older one, for the tools used were similar to the ones we use now.

Now we come to the one type of furniture that seems to be offered most frequently in America today. Oak is everywhere. Oak is king in the cities. Up here in New England we used to see seven to ten truckers at every country auction trying to fill their rigs for the trip south. Now there are often only a couple. It's not cheap even here anymore. We used to think it was absurd that city people would pay $1200 for an oak roll-top desk; now we just nod understandingly when that price is realized at the little New Hampshire auction.

The problem with oak, and even wicker furniture and brass beds, is that so much of it is being reproduced and restored. I visited an oak dealer's back room where there was row after row of disassembled furniture parts. His crew of helpers was busy replacing tops to small commodes, fixing drawers, putting new pulls on drawers, cutting legs off junk chairs to fit under china closets — replacing, renewing, restoring, and in general making silk purses out of sows' ears. Brass-bed parts waiting assembly hung from the walls. Two workers were busy fixing broken wicker furniture. Another wielded a spray gun that applied the much desired white paint to the wicker.

Most of his furniture goes to the South. Some shows up at local auctions. Nearly none gets offered to local retail shops. This is where he buys the damaged pieces that go into the back room. How do you deal with this merchandise? Simple.

If it's as cheap as a piece of new furniture, if you can use it in your home, and if you like it, then buy it. Look it over. Is it solid? Do you like the finish? Most oak is finished in orange shellac or satin polyurethane. The polyurethane will repel stains, especially alcohol, better.

Oak furniture is one type you should check out in a dealer's showroom, the Sears catalogue, and the new-furniture store before doing any heavy bidding at an auction. Prices often vary widely.

In all the periods described, there's yet one other type of furniture that was being produced. Outside of the cities, outside of the major cabinetmaking areas, the people who lived in the country made furniture, too: country, or primitive or rural, furniture, which is just as valid as the highly sought-after city examples. Country furniture reflected the styles of the cities by sometimes copying the fancy pieces, but it almost always revealed its country origins. We find it made in pine and maple instead of mahogany. We see red, blue, and yellow paint instead of walnut or maple veneer. We see form rather than ornamentation.

In the early 1970s, collectors began to discover country furniture. It sold well even before then, but not for the prices it would bring by the '80s. Today the best examples of country furniture bring astronomical prices. In the early 1970s, I saw a "mammy's bench" (a rocking bench with back and arms and a rail to keep the baby from falling out) with all its original paint selling for $600. A similar piece sold in 1980 for over $3000. Sets of painted country pine chairs, six to a set, brought $50 each at the better auctions in the '70s. Now they bring $200 each and more.

One confusing facet of these country pieces is that often a piece of furniture will turn up in a style that is easily recognizable but way out of period. We may find a Hepplewhite sideboard in rural Maryland that is completely original but which we know because of conclusive evidence (such as a cabinetmaker's signature) was made in 1850. We say it shouldn't have been made after 1810 but we know it was.

Is it a reproduction? Not by an inch. It was made by a

country cabinetmaker who was working with a style he preferred or remembered. Some Queen Anne designs have emerged that were made well into the Chippendale era. We call these pieces survival design pieces.

We also find examples of early furniture, such as Queen Anne, that were decorated several years after their origin. A tall chest of drawers made in 1750 might be completely covered with the fanciful painting that we associate with the early nineteenth century. No one in his right mind would remove this finish. The piece is doubly important: as an example of Queen Anne furniture and as an example of folk art.

Country furniture often showed none of the stylistic features of the prevalent styles. It simply served a function. The crudest, or most primitive, pieces were made from available materials such as a log, shaped and hollowed into a chair.

We find the country counterpart of the city Hepplewhite lamp stand with legs half again as thick. We see crudely nailed joints instead of the precise dovetailing of the experienced cabinetmaker.

Windsor chairs fit neatly in somewhere between country and city furniture. They were made in both places, and they fit perfectly well into a country setting. We find they were made in rural areas as well as in the big-city centers of manufacture such as Philadelphia. Windsors were being made as early as 1720 (Queen Anne era) and all the way up to 1820 (late Sheraton). One characteristic of all Windsors is that they have spindles running vertically in the back of the chair. Seats are solid, usually quite thick, and made from one piece of wood, not several pieces glued together. Early Windsors have highly turned legs. Later chairs have what are known as bamboo turnings, which resemble actual pieces of bamboo with a swelling at the scored lines.

Because of the desirability of Windsor chairs, sellers will go to extremes to save them. A common practice is to "end them out." This is a process of adding new wood to the bottoms of the legs to bring the chair up to practical height. It's entirely ethical if the buyer is aware of it. Not quite so ethical is replacing the entire chair structure below the seat.

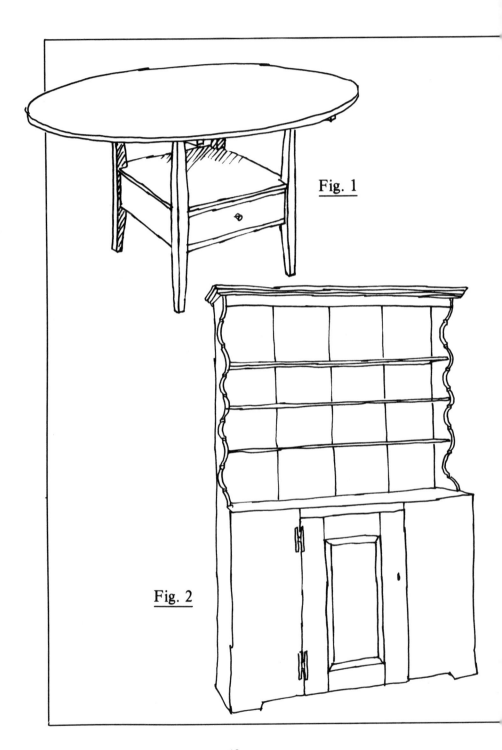

Fig. 1

Fig. 2

48

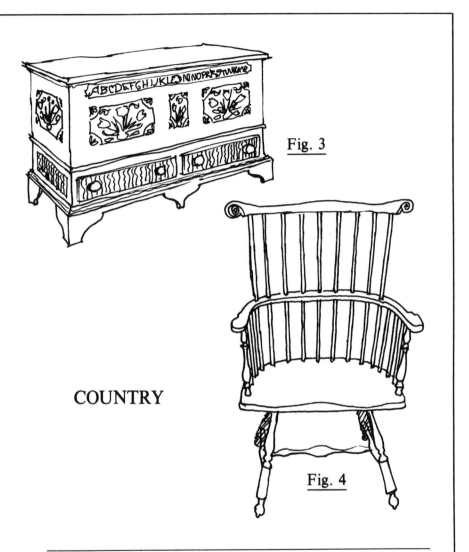

Fig. 3

COUNTRY

Fig. 4

1. Oval-top hutch or chair table. The top swings up to make the base into a chair. Look for original paint and top. 2. Scrolled-side pine cupboard from Massachusetts. These are often faked. The top should be the same age as the base and there should be no signs that the scroll cutouts were recently done. 3. Pennsylvania paint-decorated blanket chest on bracket base. Beware of repainted examples; there are quite a few around. 4. Pennsylvania comb-back Windsor armchair. Note the width of the seat and the carved ears at the ends of the comb.

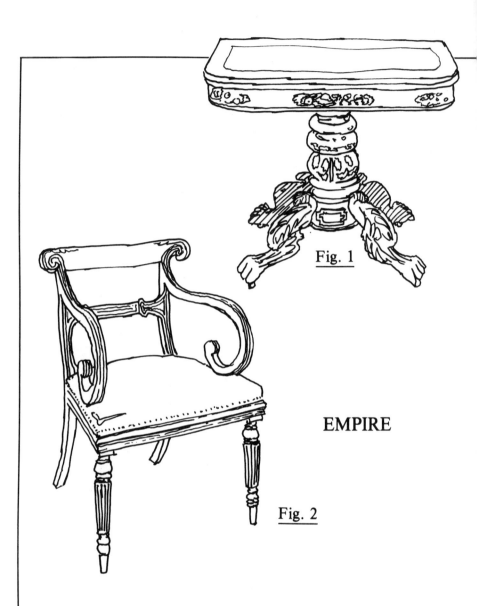

Fig. 1

EMPIRE

Fig. 2

1. Mahogany gaming table with carved knees and claw feet. Stenciled on the skirt and center pedestal. 2. Mahogany armchair with upholstered seat. The reeded legs are reminiscent of the Sheraton era. Scrolled arms and vigorous carving make this chair of the 1830s a fine example of the Empire era. 3. Boston chest of pine construction with walnut or mahogany veneer. 4. Grecian-revival couch of 1820-1835 exhibiting the best characteristics of the furniture of the Empire period.

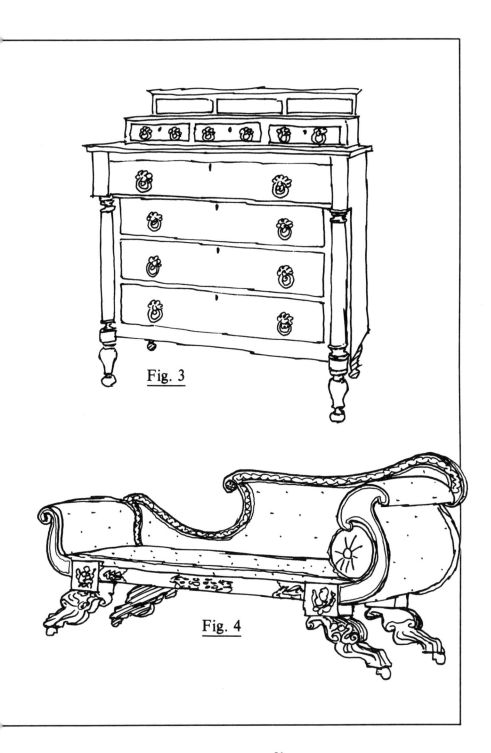

Fig. 3

Fig. 4

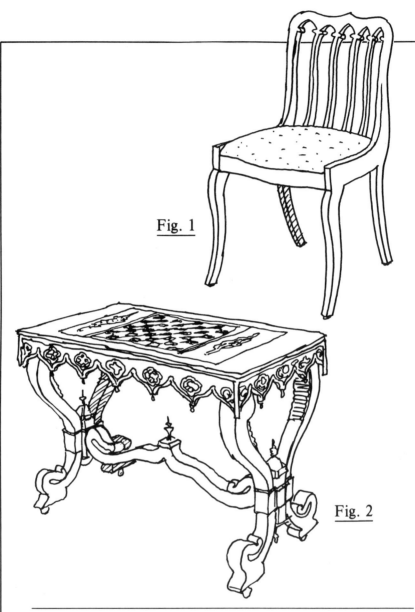

Fig. 1

Fig. 2

1. Gothic-revival sidechair of mahogany, from the period 1840-1850. Note the Gothic arches at the crest of the back. 2. Gothic-revival mahogany gaming table with inset gaming board of slate. Gothic arches along the skirt. 3. Armchair of the 1868-1869 period, showing the French influence. 4. Renaissance revival cabinet of monumental scale built around 1870-1875. Nearly seven feet tall, it fit well in the era's high-ceilinged houses.

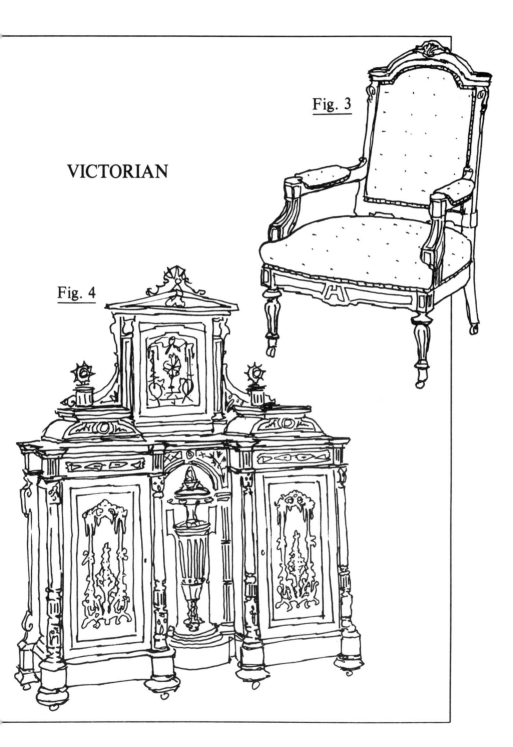

Fig. 3

VICTORIAN

Fig. 4

I attended an auction a while ago that featured over twenty Windsors, and not one chair was composed of all original parts. If the whole base hadn't been replaced, then the stretchers between the legs had been. Quite a few chairs had at one point been armed chairs, and now the only evidence of their former state was the plugs in the seats and backs.

Look over a Windsor chair closely. Look for those plugs in the seat and back. See if the legs fit the holes in the underside of the seat. Look for evidence of filled-in holes, stretchers that don't match the legs, patches on the seat, evidence of wood filler. You'll be surprised how many times you find these things.

Geographic areas have their idiosyncrasies. In New England in the first half of the nineteenth century, the simple country pine furniture was often decorated with a simulated grain painting. Using various objects ranging from brushes to feathers to wads of clay, this decoration soon evolved from simply a painted copy of a fancy grain pattern on the base color into extremely beautiful, patterned decorations. Often in vivid colors, these pieces are most desirable as expressions of American folk art.

Southern furniture was often left unpainted, and the beauty of the angular lines of a piece, combined with the natural graining, made it distinctive.

The Pennsylvania Dutch (in reality, German) people produced distinctively painted furniture that was both gaudy and beautiful. Vases of flowers, borders of leaves, and bright colors were featured.

Furniture of the Southwest and West was often simple, sturdy, and functional. This early regional furniture is distinctive and highly sought after in the area in which it was produced. The Mexican influence is easily discernible.

When the boom in country furniture began, the fakers were quick to notice. An ordinary piece could be transformed into a spectacular piece with the addition of some appropriately colored paint. The first examples I saw were crude and didn't fool anybody who'd handled the real stuff, but they got better.

I've been stung by false paint. My former partner and I were at a prestigious indoor show on opening morning one cold winter day. Just about the first ones in the door, we walked from booth to booth examining the offerings. The early child's chair just jumped out and hit me in the eye. Oak, pegged together, a bit shaky, with paneled back, scratch-molding decoration, it was a fine example of Pilgrim Century style.

My partner and I argued. The price was $60 and in those early years that was about the extent of our checking account. I was convinced it was a great piece but he was right, too; children's chairs were hard items to sell.

Finally we passed on to other booths. At last we narrowed our contemplated purchase down to three items: an early stenciled sleigh (small and attractive), a black-and-red decorated Vermont blanket box (because I'd just read an article about Vermont decorated furniture), and the child's chair (which I was holding out for). When we went back to look the chair over again, it was no longer there. The dealer told us which dealer had bought it and we trudged over to his booth. I was becoming more convinced than ever to buy it.

There it sat, but now we were looking at a price tag of $225. It was out of reach for us and as we watched, a collector eagerly bought it. All of the transactions happened within one half hour of the show's opening, and we didn't get a single piece of the action. In fact, we did a very stupid thing. We went back and bought our second choice, which happened to be the red-and-black blanket box. Very stupid indeed, for we didn't look it over closely and the painting turned out to be — on closer examination — of much later vintage than the box itself. I think we had the damn thing for six months before we swapped it to another dealer for a broken Windsor chair.

If I had obeyed the rules I listed earlier, I wouldn't have bought the box. The paint was applied over the original red paint. Examination revealed that it was a repaint. When you find paint in scratches, over chipped areas, and in cracks, it's a repaint. Fakers can do good jobs, they can even repaint an entire piece; but once you know what an original finish looks like, you usually won't be fooled.

Furniture was meant to be used. Expect some wear — a scratch or two — and look for the effects of time. Even the best of fakers has a hard job faking this successfully. Don't get carried away by what seems a bargain.

The books in the average antiques dealer's library could put your local library to shame, but there are a few that even the beginning collector or antiques buff should own.

For styles of American furniture, one of the simplest and least expensive is *How to Know American Antique Furniture* by Robert Bishop (E.P. Dutton and Co.).

Perhaps the best single book on dating, restoring, and recognizing antique furniture is *The Easy Expert in American Antiques — Knowing, Finding, Buying, and Restoring Early American Furniture* by Moreton Marsh (J.B. Lippincott Co.).

Another good, inexpensive reference book is *Antique American Country Furniture* by Thomas M. Voss (J.B. Lippincott Co.).

The bible, no doubt, of American antiques is the photographic record compiled by Wallace Nutting in 1928 and published by Macmillan entitled *Furniture Treasury*. It is still in print.

(**Note:** Some of the books I will be recommending are out of print, but a book dealer specializing in the antiques field can usually find you a copy.)

Courtesy of Vermont Travel Division, Montpelier, Vt.

3

Auctions

THE method of disposing of someone's property by auctioning it to the highest bidder has been with mankind for a long time. Auctions were recorded by Cicero in 43 B.C., but our best description of a Roman auction comes from the writings of Juvenalis in 119 A.D. *Harper's Latin Dictionary,* copyright 1907, describes an auction of this time: "Auctions were held either in an open place, or in particular rooms or halls, called atria auctionaria, or simply atria. There was a spear (hasta) set up therein, as the legal sign of the sale, like our red flag; and the price was called out by a crier (praelo) and the article sold was adjudged to the highest bidder by the magistrate who was present. A money-broker (argentarius) was also present to note down the price and receive the money or security for it."

If you have attended an auction lately, that description has a familiar ring to it, doesn't it? We may have combined the crier and the magistrate into our modern-day auctioneer but it's a very valid description of a current auction.

Over the years there has evolved a sort of folk mythology about auctions. People don't understand them, they distrust them. I've talked to country people who smile knowingly when I mention auctions. Are auctions the strange events that some think they are? Well, let's say that no more effective device exists for separating the uninformed from their money. We dealers supposedly know all the tricks and we still get taken. I attend a minimum of seventy-five auctions a year and every now and then still shake my head and say, "Well, they got me again."

What is an auction? "It's a bunch of fools showing their stupidity in public" is one veteran auction-goer's description. "It's a place to get some real bargains" is another's. The real truth about an auction lies somewhere in the middle. An auctioneer assembles the stock to be sold, finds a place in which to sell it, sends out flyers advertising the sale to a list of previous buyers or announces the sale in the papers, sells the stock item by item to the highest bidder, collects the money, and pays the owners.

Auctioneering is a profitable business. When you can make from ten to twenty-five percent on every item sold, it's no wonder that the ranks of auctioneers are swelling. Sure, you have to pay for the advertising, hire the selling premises, provide the helpers and bookkeepers, and watch out for bad checks, but consider this: you make that percentage on stock you don't own. The higher price an item brings, the more profit for an auctioneer.

This profit potential is at the root of the tricks a dishonest auctioneer uses. Right here I should note that the vast majority of auctioneers are honest. If they want to attract a crowd week after week, they have to be. But there are always a few who are tempted — the potential profits get to them. We dealers spot the tricks, we watch the auctioneers carefully. If the merchandise they handle attracts us, we still attend their auctions but we watch them.

Let's start following an auction from the time you read the flyer or the ad in the paper. You note the auctioneer's name and the location of the sale. We'll say this is an evening auction being held at the auctioneer's own hall. In all probability the auctioneer holds regularly scheduled sales at this location. You note the lead sentence of the ad, "We announce the sale of some of the finest Victorian furniture and accessories offered in this area, being the estate of the late Mrs. Anty Quarian, together with selected additions."

What that means is that some of the pieces are from the estate of the late Mrs. Anty Quarian — how many is anyone's guess — and the rest are from various other consignors. It's not a dishonest description, most auctioneers use it. Some auctioneers really do have the bulk of their sale all from one estate. Others could have as few as ten items from the named estate. Every auctioneer needs to have enough stock to fill the hours scheduled for the sale. Often at the bottom of the ad there will appear "some additions." It means the same thing. How much of the stock listed above belongs to the estate is, again, anyone's guess.

You read the listing of items to be sold, noting pieces and descriptions. You've decided there are things in this sale you collect or are interested in. You're going to go. Note carefully the time listed for inspection. This is the one most important rule for buying at auction: NEVER BUY AT AN AUCTION IF YOU HAVEN'T INSPECTED THE MERCHANDISE. That rule should be printed in blood across our checkbook covers. Every single time I've ignored it I've paid dearly for it. You will understand why when you finish this chapter.

Cut out the ad or save the flyer, for if you have never attended an auction run by this particular auctioneer, there's a little test you can do with the announcement. You're saving it primarily because, if you're like me, you tend to forget the time of the sale, the road directions, etc. My wife still remembers the morning we got up at four o'clock, drove to the White Mountains of New Hampshire, and looked around for two hours for an auction held a week earlier.

Note the terms of the sale. Will they take your check or charge card? Auctioneers have been stung a lot by bad checks. Sometimes they will take an out-of-state check with proper identification, but it's best to assume they won't. If there is a phone number listed, you could make a call to check it out.

It's the night of the auction and you've arrived safely within the inspection period. You're planning on buying some furniture so you've borrowed your neighbor's pickup. Does it seem strange I'd tell you that? Then you've never heard someone ask, "But how do I get it home?", and the auctioneer reply, "That's your problem, buddy, but you've got to get it out of here tonight." Some auctions will let you store items overnight, others longer than that, but it's a good idea to plan on taking anything you have bought with you, and here's why.

At all auctions, when the auctioneer says "sold," title falls to you. You own the piece. You're responsible for it from that second on. If it sits out in the parking lot and is stolen, too bad. If you leave it there in the hall until the next day and the hall burns during the night, tough. The rule is, know where the item you bought is stored while you remain at the auction. Ask the auctioneer or his helpers. If it seems insecure, get it in your vehicle. Some auctions provide excellent security, nothing leaves the hall until it is paid for; others take everything outside and pile it up in the dark. Check it out.

Back to the auction and the inspection period. Now's the time you do that little test I mentioned earlier. You take your auction flyer or ad and start looking for the items you were interested in. How close do the actual items come to the descriptions in the ad? (I try to form an opinion of the auctioneer and his operation from this test.) Are the descriptions fairly accurate? If the ad lists fine period furniture and all you can find are badly refinished copies, you know something: either the auctioneer is very inexperienced or he can't be trusted in his descriptions. Anyone can make a mistake, but if the entire ad is full of superlatives that don't hold up at inspection, you've been warned.

You inspect the pieces you are interested in, using the guidelines listed earlier for dating furniture. The furniture checks out pretty well. A few repairs, but nothing major. Now you try to set the price that you are willing to pay. The subject of prices and values is so important that it deserves a chapter of its own and is discussed in Chapter 8, but for now we will assume you have some experience. You have already visited area antiques shops and know what they are asking for a marble-topped walnut drop-center bureau with a high mirror similar to the one you're looking at.

You have read the price guides and the antiques magazines, you are familiar with this piece of furniture. We will assume that in the shops in your area a similar piece is selling for $800. You know this. (If you don't, if you have no idea of the retail price for this particular piece of furniture, why don't you just sit the auction out? Watch how an auction works. Note that you'd like a piece like this one or that one. Plan to visit some shops.)

Back to business. Now, is this piece you're interested in of the same quality as the piece you saw in the shop? Is it better? Does this piece need repairs? Using the shop piece as a standard, try to value this piece up or down. There's a lot to consider. Does the shop deliver? You're going to have to move the auction piece yourself. Will the shop give you a guarantee that the piece you've bought is all original? Some will. The piece you buy at auction is at your risk.

You figure the auction piece is close enough to the shop item to be worth the same price. You like it. You go over to the bookkeeper's table and register for a bidding number. Most auctioneers require them. They will accept your check and you show your identification. Then you go back and look the bureau over again. Now a little game starts. There are two other men looking at it too.

The one kneeling in front of the bureau looks up at you. "Hi, you deal in Vicky?" You stare at him, "No — no, Vicky — what's Vicky?" He smiles at the other man. "Victorian. I saw you looking this piece over earlier, figured you were a dealer." You relax. "No, I'm just looking for a bureau and like this one." The other man gives the bureau a vigorous shake. "Too bad about this piece, huh? Sure could be in better shape." You ask, "What do you mean?" His friend answers, "This piece is shaky as hell, looks like it's all been glued up and look here," he points to the marble top, "that's all replacement marble." "Gosh thanks," you murmur, and rush off to rejoin your companion and talk over what you've just heard.

Relax. What just happened is standard practice with some dealers. They noticed your interest in a piece that they wanted. Once they ascertained that you weren't a dealer, they assumed you knew nothing about the piece. Then they tried to bad-mouth the piece so you wouldn't bid on it. Some dealers will do exactly the opposite. They are regular consignors to the auction. They will watch you examine the merchandise and when you linger over a piece they've put in, they will drift over and engage you in conversation. "Boy, isn't that a beauty? Couple of big dealers came in early to look it over, don't see them back yet. Anybody gets that for less than a thousand gets a real bargain.''

Remember, at an auction you, and only you, are the judge of how good a piece is. You have to learn to take any damning or praising of a piece with a grain of salt. It's entirely possible that what you hear is the gospel truth. I have discovered some very vital information by listening to the dealer gossip before an auction. I've also found that it cost me money by not listening to that gossip.

One day I stopped at a dealer's shop and looked over his back-room pieces. These were pieces that needed work before going out on display to his retail customers. He had a table that was really wrecked. The top was split in two, both leaves were broken from the top, and it was badly stained. He offered it to me for under $10 but I refused.

Several hours later I decided to head for a local auction. I arrived late for the inspection period and quickly perused the stock. The dealer I'd seen earlier was there talking to some friends and he motioned me over. I was too busy and just nodded. Within an hour I owned his broken-up table for eight times what he'd offered it to me for. From the back of the room I didn't recognize it when it came up for bidding. He came over to me. "I tried to tell you earlier that I'd put that table in the auction this afternoon but you were too busy. Thanks for not buying it before." All I could do was smile and admit my error.

We'll assume you discounted the negative comments about the bureau. You will stick to your $800 limit. The auction is about to start. The auctioneer takes the podium. He introduces himself and announces the conditions of the sale. You listen intently. At this auction you're lucky; they store all the sold items inside the hall so you don't have to worry about the pieces you buy being outside out of sight. Everything is sold as is, that's standard practice. Or, he will take back a piece of glass or china sold as perfect that you discover within five minutes of sale isn't in that condition. Some auctioneers do this, some don't. Some won't bother to describe the damage at all. In that case, what you bid on is what you get. The necessity of inspecting the offerings is even greater.

Now he starts. The first item up is a wall-mounted coffee grinder. He asks for a $50 opening bid. When no one responds, he lowers his asking bid to $40, then $30, then finally at $20 a hand shoots up. Now the routine goes like this: "I've got twenty, who'll make it twenty-five, give twenty-five, there's my twenty-five, give thirty, go thirty, now thirty-five, go thirty-five, give thirty-five, are you all done and in at thirty?" A pause of three seconds. "Thirty-five I've got, now forty, give forty, go forty anyone? Sold for thirty-five dollars to — your number, sir? Number twelve."

The winning bidder holds up the card or paddle with his bidding number on it when asked his number by the auctioneer. This auctioneer is an average one, he knows from experience what his crowd will pay and doesn't waste a lot of time trying to start items at high prices. He sells an item quickly when the bidding stops. Some auctioneers will beg and plead to get an extra few dollars.

One thing I've observed from all the auctions I've attended is that in the majority of cases the initial asking price for an item is pretty close to the final selling price. Most auctioneers recognize this. They say, "I don't care where it starts, it only matters where it ends." Every now and then though I run into an auctioneer who won't start an item below his asking price. If he can't get that starting bid, he'll turn to the runners (the people who bring the items up to the auctioneer and out to the bidders) and say, "Pass it" or "Put it back, we'll try it later when the money people are here."

Passing, or putting back, is different from not making a reserve price. A consignor has brought the auction house a piece that the consignor particularly values. The auction house would like to handle the sale of that piece so they set a minimum value, or reserve, on the piece. They won't sell the item for a price under that reserve. Smaller houses usually won't accept reserves. It slows down an auction to accept bidding on a piece that doesn't make its reserve. One finds the practice more often confined to the city or to the larger auction houses.

Sometimes, but not always, auctioneers pass, or put back, stock because the auctioneer himself owns the piece being auctioned. Many auctioneers buy consignors' stock outright. Someone shows up with a station-wagon load of stuff and the auctioneer or one of his staff looks it over.

"Well, it isn't a bad load, not great, but not bad. Should bring at least two hundred. Tell you what I can do. Do you need the cash now? It'll bring two hundred maybe, minus the twenty percent commission, that's one sixty. I'll give you one fifty right now."

The consignor is in a difficult quandary. A lot depends on the auctioneer. If the consignor has left stock with this auctioneer before and realized good prices for the merchandise, I'd say he should consign it and take a chance. But, some auctioneers have a thing about people who won't take their offers. The stock doesn't get advertised, the auctioneer doesn't work as hard digging bids out of the crowd on the stuff, the consignor's lot always seems to come up at the end of the auction when most of the crowd has left.

A friend of mine watched this happen to him so often that he no longer consigns anything. He sells to the auctioneer now and he makes more money. Not all auctioneers are like this, but out in the country a fair percentage still are.

Some auctioneers make a point of telling the crowd, "We don't own anything in this sale," or they print in their ads, "The auction house owns no merchandise in this sale." They are the exceptions. Most auctioneers own some of the stock being auctioned.

Finally, the marble-topped bureau you've waited for comes up to the auction block. The auctioneer describes it in glowing terms. Superlatives flow from his mouth like water, finally culminating in, "This piece sat proudly for years in Mrs. Anty Quarian's dressing room." You wonder silently if you should upgrade your $800 limit. Don't. It doesn't matter where the piece sat. Except in a very few cases, the matter of who owned a piece previously has no bearing on the value of the piece.

The exception to this rule is a piece that has been photographed and exhibited as part of a famous collection. Even that piece should have such spectacular characteristics or qualities that it is recognizable as the photographed piece. An ordinary piece of machine-made manufacture such as this Victorian bureau can't qualify. You might be interested in the former owner but don't expect the next buyer to be.

The auctioneer asks for a $1000 opening bid. No one responds. He lowers to $800, then $600. From the back of the hall comes a shouted "five hundred." The auctioneer asks for $600, you raise your hand. "I've got six, now seven, go seven, I've got seven, now eight, sir?" You're out. The $700 bid came from the back of the room. It's up to you to give the $800 bid. If you do, will the bidder in the back raise it? You might lose the bureau. How about a $50 raise on the $700 bid? You make a horizontal swipe of the air in front of you with your hand extended and parallel to the floor. This is common auction English. You are drawing the slash in one-half. The auctioneer knows what you're bidding. "I've got seven fifty, didn't think of it, thank you, sir, now eight, go eight, give eight. No advance on seven fifty? It's going for seven fifty. Going once — going twice — gone! Your number, sir? Sold to number ten, seven hundred and fifty dollars."

Congratulations! You bought the piece you wanted, didn't go over your limit, and didn't make a fool of yourself. What if the other bidder had come back on the $800 bid? Then it would have been back to you for $850. But you know where there is a similar piece for $800. Stick to your limit. Know why you set a limit. Be realistic at your limit.

You wait a while longer, but the other items you were interested in go for more than you were willing to pay. You go up to the bookkeeper and pay your bill. This was a small auction and your bill only had the state sales tax added. Most of the city auctions and some of the country ones have gone to the ten percent added buyer's premium. This means that whatever you buy has ten percent added to it.

These auctions went to this English "ten and ten" system to attract quality merchandise from the consignors. A consignor pays ten percent to the auctioneer and the buyer makes up the other ten percent to give the auction house its twenty-percent commission. The auction business in the cities is an intensely competitive one. Lowering the consignor's commission to ten percent has attracted some quality offerings because the consignor now gets a full ninety percent of the sales price.

The auctioneer running a regularly scheduled auction has the problem of attracting enough merchandise to keep going. Some will advertise, others have a regular crew of pickers who attend rival auctions to pick up items that will sell better at theirs. Sometimes these pickers get their signals crossed.

We were treated one night to the spectacle of an auctioneer and his picker frantically competing for an oak china closet at a rival's auction. The hall was jammed and they were packed in the dense crowd at the back of the hall but on opposite sides. The auctioneer conducting the sale just smiled and let the bids mount. Finally the other auctioneer dropped out and glared furiously in the direction of the winning bid. The auctioneer on the podium called out the winning bidder's number, then paused, "Do you know the underbidder over there? Wave your hands, gentlemen." The picker waved numbly to his auctioneer while the rest of us roared.

There are a lot of tricks an auctioneer can use to raise bids. Some of them are legal, a few aren't. False descriptions are legal. If you believe everything an auctioneer says, you could be in serious trouble. Quite often an auctioneer simply doesn't know when a piece is a reproduction or has serious problems. You have to be the judge of how good a piece is.

When the auctioneer states that everything sold is sold as is, where is, it means just that. No matter how he describes an item, there is no guarantee or warranty given. If he describes a piece of furniture as late-eighteenth-century Hepplewhite and you buy it and find it's a late-nineteenth-century copy, you have no legal comeback. His verbal description is worth exactly nothing. The only exception to this is the guarantee given by a very few large auction houses such as Sotheby Parke-Bernet Inc. Even their guarantees are extremely limited.

Also legal is the practice of "loading" an auction. Auctioneers know that those auctions held during the fair-weather months at outdoor locations attract a higher paying crowd. Besides the tourists who can be counted on to show up, dealers come because they expect an on-site location to turn up fresh goodies from a previously untapped source. So, many auctioneers take the stock they have been buying privately and add it to the house's contents — this is referred to as loading.

How much they dare to add depends on the auctioneer's cupidity. I attended one auction that revealed eleven beds among the contents of a six-room house. It was possible to have that many if the attic had never been unloaded, but these were all of the same vintage. Very suspicious.

In another instance, a dealer who had decided to go out of business bought a house in a rural area over two hundred miles away from his shop. Off went all the stickers on the furniture, and the stock was trucked up to the bare house. Quite a few auctioneers turned down his offer to handle the sale, but he finally found one who would. I saw the flyer. The pieces had been photographed strategically spotted around the house. It was a darn good-looking ad. Nothing was mentioned about his former occupation or the fact that the pieces had only been in the house for a week. I later heard the prices were high.

Remember, you are buying only the piece you are bidding on, nothing else, no story, no location of the sale, just that piece.

Another practice that is perfectly legal and honest in the hands of the ethical auctioneer but that lends itself to a different bent in the hands of the dishonest is the left-bid practice. A bidder attends the preview, sees an item he wishes to bid on, but can't be at the auction. Some auctioneers permit this bidder to leave a bid, then have an employee of the auction house execute this absentee, or left, bid. Auction-house practices vary, but in general the bidding will start at half of the left bid.

An unethical auctioneer knows he holds a guaranteed price in his hands. He simply informs another house employee or confederate to raise the bidding on that item to the left-bid level. If you plan to leave left bids many times with an auction house, you should attend a few of the auctions to see how they execute left bids. Better still, count on paying the full bid you leave.

The left-bid practice really gets a working over by a few auctioneers. These guys have found a way to protect the items they own personally. We'll say the auctioneer has bought a very desirable tiger maple slant-front country desk from a private home. He paid a bargain $500 for it. He advertises it for one of his weekly auctions. That night a rival is holding an auction twenty miles away. He scans his own crowd; all the important buyers must be at his competitor's auction. He doesn't see anyone who will go the $4000 minimum the desk should bring. He has a highly advertised on-site house auction coming up in two months. He decides he'd like to save the desk for that auction rather than see it sold cheaply here.

He tells the employee bidding for the book (the list of left bids), "Protect that desk; if we don't have a bid of at least four thousand, bid on the desk." A local dealer in the audience opens the bidding for $1000, the employee bids $1500, the local dealer hesitates, then comes back with $1750. The employee raises his hand at the call for $2000. The dealer drops out and the auctioneer still owns the desk. Two months later you attend the house auction. A buyer pays $4000 for the desk. If you had the guts to ask the auctioneer who the consignor was, you would probably hear, "None of your damn business!" He'd be right, of course. The only way you could prove he'd done it would be to examine his books. If he's sharp, he might carry the name of a fictitious consignor and buyer on the books.

Sometimes auctioneers will even use the left-bid trick to pick up a consignor's item that is dropping out or going for a ridiculously low price. The same auctioneer has a choice consignment of early Wedgwood pieces at his weekly auction. He doesn't think his weekly buyers will appreciate their value. He arranges for "the book" to bid up to half of their value. If a floor bidder goes over that price, he gets the item. Those that go for under the price get sold to "the book," or the auctioneer. He deducts his commission from the prices realized, the consignor gets his check, and the auctioneer owns some choice Wedgwood for perhaps thirty percent of their retail value. If the auctioneer owns a retail shop, you may spot them there. If not, they may make their way into one of his more prestigious auctions.

There is no way to tell if an auctioneer is abusing the left-bid system without attending his auctions regularly. Even then, if he's clever and does his paperwork scrupulously, it's a hard thing to prove. You may suspect he does abuse the system, but it's best to keep quiet. Lawsuits are very expensive. Just be content to know that here is an auctioneer not to be trusted.

A much more flagrant and often abused practice is the bouncing-a-bid-off-the-wall ploy, sometimes called pulling a bid out of the air. This is something even a beginning auction-goer can spot. The auctioneer will use it to up the bids of an excited bidder.

A piece has started at a very low opening bid, the bidder shows his excitement, waving his hands frantically. The auctioneer doesn't see another bidder but to him it's obvious this one will go higher. He bounces the next bid off the wall, pointing to a nonexistent bidder. "Twenty, twenty, I've got twenty, who'll go thirty, I've got thirty, who'll go forty?" He's back to his original bidder for $40, the $30 came off the wall or out of the air.

Auctioneers are very adept at knowing how far a bidder will go. He's guessed $40 and he's right. Sometimes a new bidder will come in at this point and, if the piece goes over one bidder's limit, it can be assumed the new bidder was bidding all along. It's tricky to tell where bids do come from. Some bidders wave their bidding numbers, others just nod.

If an auctioneer runs a bidder up over his limit by bouncing bids off the wall and no other bidder surfaces, he'll usually cover himself by saying something like, "I've got eighty, who'll go ninety, ninety, looking for ninety, are you out, Madam? I think you can get it for ninety. No? Ninety, anyone? Sold back there for eighty. Who's my eighty dollar bidder? Someone back there was bidding. Come on, who was bidding back there? I saw a hand. Well then, sold to you, Madam, for seventy, you were the under-bidder.''

Now you are in a quandary. Yes, you did bid $70, but was there even a real $60 bidder? I usually take it the first time it happens in an auction. The second time in one auction I refuse the piece and don't bid again.

Auctioneers use this tactic on grudge rivals or competing dealers, too. They usually know all the gossip about relationships between their dealer customers. They'll bounce a bid off a competitor, or in the vicinity of a competitor, to get the next bid from a rival.

Watch for an auctioneer who consistently has to back down from a winning bid to the under-bidder. The odds are he is bouncing them off the wall. Every auctioneer will miss or lose a bidder occasionally, but several times an auction is too much.

The auctioneer has another variation of this trick to use. He can simply station a confederate in the back of the hall with his bidding number prominently displayed in a front pocket. He will bounce the bids off this confederate and if you drop out, he'll announce the winning number of the confederate. If you turn around to spot the winning bid, there stands a real bidder.

Be suspicious when a lot of stock gets sold to one of the auctioneer's friends. Be doubly suspicious when this same stock shows up again in another auction by the same auctioneer. Once an item comes up to the auction block, forget about watching it; watch the bidders, see where the bids come from. You've already inspected the merchandise, now you're watching the auctioneer and the bidders. It will take a while to discover if a particular auctioneer cheats, so don't expect to attend one auction and come away with a conclusive opinion. Sometimes, if you listen to the regulars talk, you will pick up a particular auctioneer's tricks. Ask a dealer you trust what he thinks of the auctioneer.

When you were getting that bureau you bought out to the

parking lot and your truck, did you notice a group of men gathered around the front of a van and holding handfuls of cash? If you did, what you probably saw was the "pool" settling up. What's a pool? The pool, or ring, is the answer of certain groups of dealers to rising auction prices. A pool consists of a group of dealers who agree not to compete with each other at an auction. They look over the merchandise, decide on the pieces they want, then agree to not bid against each other on those pieces.

Sometimes only one member will do the bidding, other times anyone can open the bidding; the others will stay out. If a pool is large enough, or there isn't much competition from the rest of the bidders, the pool can make some very good buys. Later they re-auction the items bought among themselves and divide the profits.

What kind of a profit can a pool make? Let's look at a typical example. The auction is a full house lot. Among the furniture are six good pieces of Victorian walnut. Four dealers look over the crowd. There are a couple of other auction-house owners, a smattering of tourists, and a few local small dealers. The four dealers decide to form a pool.

The first piece they want is a high walnut bed. A local dealer opens the bidding at $50. The pool member bids $75. The local dealer goes $100. The pool comes back with $125 and gets the bed. The local dealer looks back to see where the bid came from and recognizes the group of four as probably a pool. He might even have sold to some of the members in the past. When the next item comes up he doesn't bid. He sees the futility of bidding against people he sells to. The next piece is a marble-topped walnut table. The pool opens the bidding for $100. A private bidder goes $125, the pool comes back with $150. The auctioneer pleads for bids. The pool gets the table. The next two pieces are duck soup. There aren't any other dealers in Victorian furniture at the auction who care to compete with them. The tourists are just that.

The pool goes outside to settle up. It's bad form to do it in the auctioneer's hall. The bed that cost $125 starts the bidding, they start from there and each bids it up. One dealer is willing to pay $200 for it. That means that the pool as an entirety has just made $75. Next they bid the table they paid $150 for up to $250. The pool makes $100 on that. For simplicity's sake we'll say that the last two items are chairs and they paid $150 for the pair. They bid them up to $250 for the pair. The winning bidders put up the money for their purchases, a total of $700. They have to pay the auctioneer $425. They have $275 to divide among the four of them, or nearly $69 each. Any wonder that dealers form pools?

The lure of easy money makes for strange bedfellows. I know of one pool that formed on a winter night at a small auction that put some real rivals together. It was an all-oak auction organized by a part-time auctioneer in a very rural area. The auctioneer decided to hold down costs by scrimping on advertising, a cardinal mistake. When fewer than thirty people showed up, the ten dealers in oak furnishings present formed a pool more quickly than you could say "bankrupt."

Five of the ten pool members were truckers or dealers who trucked their stock to the South for re-auctioning. They normally were fierce rivals. The remaining members had never had a good word for each other. To top it off, the wife of one had left him to live with another of the pool members. But this night they had the action all to themselves.

The poor auctioneer knew what was happening but he couldn't do anything about it. Everything he had was invested in that one sale. He ran the auction and watched his stock sold on one bid. Oh, the pool had a heart; most of the time they bid at least as much as he'd paid for the piece, most of the time.

He doesn't run auctions anymore. He learned the hard way that if enough dealers are present who haven't joined a pool, and if enough private buyers are present at an auction, the pool can't succeed. But he didn't advertise, he didn't attract those extra people. It was an expensive lesson.

There is enough money to be made by a pool so that the members can afford to intimidate, or punish, a dealer who won't join. They can lose money on an item or more than one item to prove that they shouldn't be crossed. I've seen a pool pay over double the retail price for an item to push the point home to a stubborn dealer.

If you are being pushed by the pool, just remember your limits. It's foolish to pay too much for an item.

When you've decided to sell your collection or family heirlooms at auction, there are some basic rules to follow. Look for an auctioneer who specializes in the types of items you have to sell. If an auctioneer is well known for his auctions of Victorian furnishings, he probably wouldn't do the best job with your collection of primitive painted furniture. Some auctioneers have distinct specialties and are well followed in their fields. Try to seek out the best auctioneer for your offerings.

If you have an assortment of pieces, you still want to get the most money for them. Check out various auctioneers' ads. Would your items fit in with what the auctioneer usually sells? Does the auctioneer have a good reputation? Auctioneers' commissions are fairly standard but call more than one to check. Give the auctioneer time enough to properly advertise your offerings. Don't expect to bring him your pieces on Monday for a Wednesday auction.

Some people like to attend the auction when their pieces are sold and note every sale. This is usually not necessary. Auctioneers, even crooked auctioneers, can make enough money playing other games without fooling with the consignor's money. Being caught cheating with the consignor's money is the one sure way to lose a license. Do make sure you know when you will be paid. Some auctioneers pay within ten days, others within thirty days. Others wait until all buyers' checks clear before paying consignors.

Auctions are fun. For those of us in the antiques business, they provide a storehouse of new merchandise, a weekly meeting place, and the opportunity to see old friends, make new ones, hear the rumors, discover new trends, and renew our zeal for the whole business of antiques. Don't let the seamier side of auctions disillusion you. Just remember the rules of the game.

Courtesy of Patricia Anne Reed Antiques, Damariscotta, Me.

4

Dealers, Antiques Shops, Antiques Shows

BEFORE you visited that auction to bid on the walnut bureau you wanted, I assume you had checked out the local antiques shops. I hope the assumption is valid. You have to start somewhere with a basic price in mind. Perhaps you saw similar bureaus at low prices, even saw some with much higher prices than the $800 figure you settled on. That's common; dealers use various methods to price their stock. Some mark up a strict percentage from cost, others use price guides to set a retail price, and still others try to remember the last auction price they saw a similar piece bring.

All dealers have one thing in common however: they sell a product that has not been produced for years, and in most cases have no central warehouse to call to reorder the merchandise sold. The grocer has his stock delivered daily; the car dealer gets on the phone to the factory; the chic little boutique receives its fall line in the middle of the summer; the antiques dealer is always thinking, "Where can I get some fresh stock?"

This insecurity about where tomorrow's merchandise is coming from is only one of the dealer's headaches. Back in the days when I ran a retail shop, one of the most frequently asked questions was, "Where do you get all this stuff?" Often I got the impression that the questioner assumed that the merchandise was family leftovers.

Let's clear up some misconceptions. Antiques dealers are

like any other business people. They buy their stock, mark up to a retail price, and with the profit realized when the item sells, they pay the expenses of doing business. The sellers you see at a flea market or yard sale may or may not be dealers (sometimes it's a dealer getting rid of his lower-priced items); but if the sellers own or rent a shop, set up at an antiques show, or are in business more than a week, the odds are they are antiques dealers trying to make a living.

Dealers know you shop around for the best buy when you shop for groceries. You wait for the "white" sales when you need new sheets, you comparison-shop when the family car is on its last legs; but when you do find the item you want, you don't run to the sales clerk and make an offer lower than the price marked. Well, some of you still do this in antiques shops.

Maybe the reason people feel they can bargain in the shops is they think many of us aren't professional enough about our businesses. Very few dealers live totally off their shop profits. At the very top of the spectrum are those dealers who make the headlines. They sell to museums and affluent private collectors. Their stock is the very best, and expensive. Next come the good average dealers. They sell at shows from California to Virginia. You can see their ads in *The Magazine Antiques,* but they are rarely full page. And then we have the majority of dealers, the ones who have a working spouse, who draw Social Security or work on weekdays, and who sell on weekends.

The average dealer has another income. Given the insecurities of supply and demand and the amount of capital required to live off an antiques business, it is no wonder he does. Many of these dealers need to turn over their merchandise quickly, they can't afford to hold on to their investments for a long time. That's why they are willing to dicker.

A dealer of this type will see that you are interested in a piece but are hesitating over the price. That's when his prices waver. He may say, "Well, it's marked two hundred but I could let you have it for one seventy-five." If this happens to you and it's a piece you were thinking of buying at $200, you have a bargain. I don't like the practice, it is unprofessional, but some dealers persist in doing it.

Good dealers don't need to price chop. They have marked their stock fairly. A retail customer visiting their shops should not expect a discount for purchasing. If, over a period of time, the customer establishes a good relationship with the shop owner, who occasionally knocks down the price of a piece to this customer, that's fine. That is a friendly act and strictly a courtesy between two individuals. Because we deal in interesting and often rare items, we occasionally become friendly with our customers. That's not uncommon. A good dealer likes what he sells. A knowledgeable customer shares this feeling.

Occasionally a dealer will give a discount for a large-volume purchase. You enter a shop and discover a collection of ten painted wooden nineteenth-century checkerboards. They are priced individually. You collect game boards. Yes, you can ask, "I'm interested in the game boards, what would the price be if I took all ten?" It's a fair question. The dealer may simply add the ten prices together and give you the total. If the person you're talking to is only an employee of the shop owner, he may not be authorized to sell for a lower price. Even if you're talking to the owner, he may not want to cut what is already a fair price. On the other hand, the dealer may have bought them all as a collection and realizes the benefits of selling all ten to one customer. He may give you a much better price for the full ten. This is the only exception I can think of for asking for a discount as a retail customer. Don't try it if you are just picking up ten different items in a shop. Those items all represent a small markup to the dealer.

Dealers do discount to other dealers. Since inter-dealer sales account for up to seventy-five percent of some dealers' sales, discounting makes sense. The discounts vary. Some discount a flat ten percent, others favor a dealer price for each item. Don't ask for this dealer discount unless you really are a dealer. The amount of identification required varies from state to state. A legitimate dealer has a sales-tax number in his home state with the exception of New Hampshire. Some states won't even accept an out-of-state tax number.

When you walk into a shop for the first time, look at the overall appearance. Does the dealer care if his stock is clean? Pride in the appearance of the shop tells a lot about the owner and the stock. Are the price stickers old and faded? If the dealer hasn't priced his stock for the past year, you might find a real bargain. On the other hand, why hasn't the stock sold for a year? Is it still overpriced? Another tip. If the stickers on the merchandise are severely faded, it could be that the dealer has been offering his stock at outdoor flea markets on weekends. It didn't sell. Is it still overpriced? Is each item marked with a price? It may only be a personal preference, but I always feel uncomfortable asking the price of every item I'm interested in. Somehow the feeling comes across that the dealer doesn't want you to know the price.

Prices should not be a secret. I know the dealer paid less for the item than he is selling it for. If he didn't, the man's a lunatic. The use of elaborate codes on the price stickers only complicates matters.

Ask questions. It quickly becomes evident if the dealer knows anything about the antique you are interested in. Remember, you are the customer; you represent a potential profit in the dealer's pocket. If you are only browsing, say so. Don't waste the dealer's time if there is another seriously interested customer in the shop. He might not mind explaining the fine points of the English hunting print you think is nice, but if it means losing the customer who is seriously considering buying the set of six Pennsylvania splat-back chairs that he has had for two years, he won't be very happy.

If you have an adequate knowledge of the field you collect in, talk to the dealer about it. Ask him about a piece when you find it in his shop. If he admits that it isn't his specialty, that's fine. He's honest. If he starts using every superlative in the book and you know it's just an average piece, beware. He wants to sell you and will use any trick to do it. If the price is right, buy anyway, but file away in your head the fact that the dealer can't be trusted.

A good antiques dealer will admit ignorance when he

simply doesn't know. If something is really good, he will tell you why. If you are an occasional buyer, you are at the mercy of the dealer. You probably don't carry price guides, read antiques publications, and attend auctions weekly. So ask the dealer why the item is priced as it is. He should be able to explain the range of prices for that field, tell you what similar pieces sell for in the area, and describe any particularly good (or bad) points that make that individual piece worth what it is marked.

If the item is in the low-price field, all this is not necessary. In most cases the dealer simply bought it, tacked on his markup, and is trying to sell it. You either like it and can afford it, or you don't and can't.

There is a very good rule for both dealer and customer: if you have any doubts about a piece, don't buy it. For all the times I've regretted not buying something, there have been many more that I've cursed myself for not following that rule. The piece I'm considering is attractive but something doesn't quite sing to me. I think I can make money on it. Maybe. I walk away, think some more. Oh well, why not? Months later it still sits there. I sigh, and ask myself, "Why didn't you follow the rule?" Believe in your instincts.

A dealer learns that his best advertising is a satisfied customer. Mine returned season after season and they brought new customers with them. No matter how much advertising one does, if the goods do not hold up under the customer's scrutiny, and the prices are not fair, you cannot stay in business. Advertising lets people know what you have, and it is sometimes necessary, but customers will come back only if they are satisfied. Shops are like museums sometimes; people will be interested in your displays, return several times to look without buying anything, and then one day inform you they have started collecting because of an interest born in your shop. It's a satisfying feeling.

Let's look at a typical day for an average shop owner. Typical, that is, in that I've placed him in a rural area, near a large New England city, in a three-room shop that is part of his own house. He's open year-round except for vacations, when he's usually buying.

It's an early-summer morning. Our dealer breakfasts and goes downstairs to the shop. He pulls his wife's car around to the shop parking lot and puts up the "open" signs. There's a reason for the car in the parking lot. So many dealers leave an open sign up permanently that some customers have come to disbelieve them. A car in the parking lot signifies that someone is really there. He checks his doors and windows to make sure no one has broken in during the night. Thefts are becoming more of a problem for dealers nowadays, even in rural New England.

The shop is secure. He empties the ashtrays, sweeps the floor, does a little dusting, pours the first of many cups of coffee. He checks the merchandise as he cleans; this morning he's lucky, everything is there. Depending on how many small items he carries, thefts run from once a month to once a week. During the heights of heavy tourist seasons he's had thefts at the rate of once a day.

Out come the sales books and inventory records. Every item sold yesterday has to be entered, along with whether a sales tax was collected or not. If a sale was made to another dealer, that has to be recorded, too. Sales have to be noted in the inventory book so he won't be paying an inventory tax on a nonexistent item.

Our shop owner goes out to his station wagon to bring in the pieces he purchased at auction the night before. The auction started at six o'clock and he was there at five. Missing the inspection period before an auction is a cardinal sin.

He thinks about the black walnut roll-top desk that he had wanted. Advertised as being in prime condition, it had proved under close scrutiny to be a married piece. In itself that wouldn't have hurt, but the top had been cut down to fit the bottom. And to top it off, the consignor, or someone at the auction barn, had discovered it coming apart and applied white glue to the joints; lots of white glue that ran down the black walnut.

When the bidding on the desk passed the $1000 mark, he had settled back against the wall and thought, "Let the truckers take it. If they can get twelve hundred for it in New York or the South, they're welcome to it. I run a retail shop in New England. I'd sit on that for a year at that price!''

He brings in the Victorian silk patchwork crazy quilt he bought. The patches are bright, they are on black velvet, and the quilt is totally hand-sewn. The bidding on it was brisk and he had to go to $175 to get it. More than he wanted to pay, but then, it's colorful, attractive, and only very slightly damaged. There is a place on the wall in the second room that is perfect for it. Putting it up, he thinks of a fair retail price. ''I've never sold one for more than two thirty-five. How long do I want to keep it around? If I put two and a quarter on it, it should go.'' He puts on a sticker with the price $225 and his inventory number.

A few minutes later the first customer of the day comes in. She's a shop owner from New York City. She stops at those shops where she has had good buys before. She knows her customers' tastes, she is a careful buyer. She likes quilts.

''You have two and a quarter on the crazy quilt; what's my price?''

He thinks. He only bought it last night, should he wait and see if he can sell it at retail? On the other hand, if the price is right, she will take it now and he can turn the money over on something else. He gives her the dealer discount.

''I just bought it. For you, two hundred.''

''Hm-m-m. OK.''

And that's the way it really is. If you are a country dealer, you have to turn the stock over to survive.

Until afternoon, she's the only customer who's been in the shop. At about two he sees a station wagon pull into the parking lot. It has in-state plates. The couple are in their late sixties. They refuse his offer of help and murmur something about just looking. He watches them pause at the ironstone bowl-and-pitcher set in the second room, read the price, and look hard at each other. He knows what's happening.

Either they have just sold a bowl-and-pitcher set to another dealer or they are getting ready to sell theirs. He wonders which. If they are getting ready to sell, will they show up at the local flea market on Sunday with his retail price on the set? If they do, they will be in for a long wait. He's had his for four months now.

He watches them price other items in the shop and decides they're getting ready to sell. He mentions to them that he buys antiques, too. They look at each other. "Oh, we don't have anything we want to sell yet," she says. They leave and he wonders how long they will try to sell their items before coming back and how many pieces he'll ever see.

Just before closing he sells the only refinished piece of furniture in the shop, a pine drop-leaf table that had been stripped, and then finished with satin polyurethane. His wife had bought it from a friend who was moving, and paid $100 for it. He'd agreed it was worth the hundred but he disliked the piece because of the finish. Some shops sell nothing but refinished furniture, but he is a purist. Besides that, he had always thought it stood out like a sore thumb in the shop. The young couple love the piece, though, and don't haggle a second over the $175 price tag. He will have to eat a lot of crow when his wife finds out. He closes the shop down, checks the locks, and goes upstairs with the $375 worth of receipts for the day. Most of it will be reinvested, some will go toward the overdue bills, a little will pay for the dinner he owes his wife.

Where does the stock come from? Surprisingly, there are a few warehouses of antiques. They are almost always located in the large cities and invariably offer European antiques. This merchandise arrives in container loads; it's sold to dealers only and often there is a minimum buying quantity. If you live near a city and know a shop that sells mostly European antiques, the stock probably came from a warehouse.

Outside of this one exception dealers are on their own as to replenishing supply. Some dealers haunt the auction halls, competing against other dealers and often against the very retail customers to whom they later offer the merchandise. Because of this fact, quite a few dealers prefer to attend auctions outside of their own area. Some dealers don't like to be seen paying $200 for a piece at auction, then have people who attended the auction observe the $300 price tag in the shop.

It's a needless worry. Everyone knows a dealer will mark up an item he buys. If he gets a spectacular buy, he has more of a markup. Some dealers only mark up twenty percent, but I have yet to see a dealer buy a legitimate $1000 retail-price item for $100 and only mark up twenty percent if he can get $800 from another dealer. That's why dealers attend auctions. They hope they can make a spectacular buy.

Dealers buy from other dealers. One dealer may live in an area that pulls hot buyers for country items. He buys at auction a quantity of Staffordshire figurines at a low price. Another dealer from a metropolitan area in the South stops in, a dealer who customarily sells any piece of Staffordshire she can lay her hands on at very high prices. You can guess what's going to happen. Exit a happy dealer from the South.

Later the first dealer travels South. He buys a truckload of country items from dealers there. They all move well from his own shop up north. This moving of stock from shop to shop, East to West, North to South, can happen even within one town. I sell furniture, another dealer nearby sells glass; she buys from me and I buy from her.

Dealers also buy from pickers, who know what the dealers specialize in. They travel from shop to shop, attend the auctions, watch the sales, make the contacts with private sellers — always knowing that they have to buy low enough to sell to the dealer for a profit and still allow the dealer to profit. Pickers give up the potential retail profits for the freedom of not having to carry large inventories. Some dealers are wary of pickers. They have been stung by pickers selling stolen merchandise.

Dealers are always susceptible to getting stuck with stolen goods. No dealer wants to own a stolen piece but because he has to replace the sold merchandise, he must buy when he can. When someone shows up at the shop and offers merchandise that the dealer can profit on, the dealer usually says yes. He tries to protect himself. He usually insists on a receipt and pays by check. When the seller won't give a receipt and insists on cash, it's a sure tip-off that something is wrong. Some states require dealers to keep records of their purchases, noting names and identifications of the sellers.

It's possible to play by all the rules and still get stuck with stolen merchandise. While I was running a shop, I ended up with stolen goods even with receipts and payments by check. A young man drove up one day and explained that he was interested in selling some antiques. He was a local resident. He sold me several mid-nineteenth century daguerreotype cases with their early photos intact. After giving me a receipt and accepting my check he explained that he was out of work and asked if I would be interested in buying other antiques?

Well, what would any dealer say? I said yes. He was in twice the next week. Both times he sold me small lots, good salable items that I promptly resold. He explained that he was going out into the country visiting people he knew and buying from them.

Finally he stopped by and said he was in a quandary. He'd seen a full-size brass bed in one house. "How much shall I offer for it?" I could have said I'd give him a profit if he'd take me to see the bed, but I didn't want to cut him out. I told him how much I'd pay and how much I'd sell the bed for. I wanted to keep him as a picker. My markup was no secret.

He was back the next day and he had the bed. I got the receipt and gave him the check. The bed received a super polishing and was proudly displayed on the shop porch. It was sold three days later. Two days after that I was visited by the state police. My new "picker" was discovered in the act at his warehouse — a locked-up summer cottage.

I located my buyer from my sales slip, the police confiscated the bed, I refunded in full the buyer's price, and was out the money I'd given the picker. He received a seven-day suspended sentence and a $30 fine.

It was quite a while before I bought from a picker again, but eventually someone brought in some super stock and I bought it. I was lucky, for that earlier incident was the only time I ever got taken by a picker.

Every dealer is susceptible. The tip-off is when merchandise is extremely cheap and the seller wants cash. A good dealer can't afford to be known for handling stolen goods. If we get stuck, we take care of you, our customers. We refund your money, apologize, cooperate with the authorities, so don't condemn us if it does happen. It is in the very nature of this business. The stock has to come from somewhere; sometimes — thank God, it's rare — it's stolen.

Dealers also buy from private parties, meaning you. How do you sell something to a dealer? To start with, do you have any idea of the item's worth? There are several ways to find out its value. You could check any of the many price guides on the market. Remember that what you will find is the retail price, not the price you can get from a dealer for your offering. You could check and see what a similar piece is selling for in area antiques shops. You could attend several antiques shows and price similar pieces. You could also obtain a paid appraisal (see Chapter 9).

Let's say you have a nice flow-blue covered bowl made in England about 1850 that you want to sell. ("Flow-blue" refers to the blue decoration under the glaze, used on pieces of china produced in England, that ran when the piece was fired.) Is yours in good shape? Does it have any chips? Is it discolored or stained? Condition makes a difference in price. We'll say yours is equal to the others you've seen for sale.

If you want to offer yours to a shop, be sure the shop sells that kind of merchandise. You'd be surprised how many people offer merchandise to shops that have no desire to sell the type offered.

If you have not seen similar pieces in the shops with which you are familiar, check the Yellow Pages in your telephone directory. Look in the classified section of your paper. Once you've decided on dealers to offer your piece to, call them.

You may find at this point that they will want to come to you. If you have other pieces that you are considering selling, this could be acceptable. There are possible problems here though. As a dealer (or picker), I love getting into your house. If I can't buy the item you're offering, I can frequently find something else. But for you, the seller, I'd recommend bringing that first item to the dealer.

Be sure you go to a good, reputable dealer. The vast majority are honest but there are a few bad apples out there. Pick a dealer who advertises and has a good reputation. Don't invite trouble by spreading the word that you have a house full of antiques you'd like to unload; instead, see how your first contact with the dealer goes. If you like the dealer and trust him, then invite him to your house.

When you show up at the dealer's with your bowl, you'll probably be asked what you want for it. Most dealers don't make offers. They consider making an offer tantamount to giving a free appraisal. They are also hoping you want far less than they can sell the piece for. If the dealer has an interest in your piece and does make an offer, it will probably be in the range of fifty percent to seventy percent of what he estimates will be its retail price. If the piece you are offering is of exceptional quality, is highly salable, or really excites the dealer, he might go as high as eighty percent of retail. For the dealer to go that high, he has to truly desire the piece or know where he can immediately sell it for a profit.

The dealer you've shown your bowl to doesn't make an offer. He looks the bowl over carefully. He checks the cover for rim flicks (small nicks around the outer edge), he looks for concealed hairline cracks, and finally he's satisfied. He asks how much you want for it. You've checked the price guides and seen similar bowls priced at $100. You've also visited other shops and a couple of antiques shows. Similar pieces you've seen range from $85 to $100.

Be realistic. You're not in love with the piece. It is a family heirloom but doesn't fit in with anything you have now. If it does have vast sentimental value, you shouldn't be selling it. No amount of money is going to fill that void. Offer a piece that you can bear to sell. An antiques shop is not a pawn shop. A dealer is not going to hold a piece until you can buy it back. It may be resold before you reach your car.

You know your piece is perfect but it's not the most spectacular in the world. It's just good, salable merchandise. If $100 is the top price you've seen, go for fifty percent of it. The dealer knows the top price, too. He knows he can stay under the top price and still make a profit on your offering. The dealer might still refuse, for which there could be several reasons.

He might find that this item is a slow mover in his shop. He might be overstocked. He might be having cash-flow problems. He might even be in a bad mood that day.

If you have accurately compared your offering to similar retail pieces and prices in your area, you should have no trouble eventually realizing this fifty percent figure. My sympathies go out to those of you trying to sell your antiques, though. I know that when you find a dealer willing to pay your price, you always wonder if you sold too cheaply.

Take heart. It hurt like hell when I started being a picker. I didn't just wonder if I'd sold too cheaply — I *knew* I had. I eventually realized that that was the only way a picker worked. He has to sell to the dealers so they can make a profit. No dealer is going to pay retail price to a picker — or even to you, for that matter — just to turn around and resell for the same retail price. You get used to it after a while.

The point is that you are selling, realizing money for an item you want to dispose of. The dealer has to hold it in his inventory, heat it, insure it, pay rent on a place to store it, and, he hopes, make a profit on it when it is sold. If you want to do all these things, become a dealer.

There is a way to realize more than this fifty percent to seventy percent of retail for your antique. If you own a really choice antique, you could do exactly what a lot of pickers do — offer it to a dealer right before an antiques show is held. Check the advertisements for an upcoming important antiques show, something like the East Side Show held in New York City in late January. See who the exhibitors are and try to match your offering with a dealer who specializes in what you're offering. Your piece should be fresh — not something you have already offered around to several other dealers. It would help to have researched the ownership of it and be able to offer this research in writing. Then, a few weeks before the show is held, offer your antique to the dealer you've chosen. Dealers doing the top shows are always on the lookout for fresh, quality stock. If your piece is truly fine, you can ask a price very near the last auction or retail price that you can match it to.

I've done this for years. When I come up with a really pristine antique from a private home, I try to tuck it away. Then, right before the good shows roll around, I have a piece to offer that no other dealer has seen. Dealers doing the prestigious shows want to attract new customers, the investment and museum buyers. A very fine piece at a quality show will sell for far more than it will in a shop. Just be sure to offer your antique to a dealer far enough in advance of the show so that he will have time to advertise it.

For many dealers the antiques-show circuit is the answer to those slow, off-season months. Instead of sitting around the shop in the middle of January waiting for an occasional customer, they sign up to exhibit their wares at a big show in Birmingham, Alabama; Concord, New Hampshire; or New York City. The shows do provide additional exposure for dealers, and serve as quite a showplace for you, the retail buyer, too. You could spend a month on the road and not see as many antique egg cups as you can find at one big-city show.

Some shows have a feature, called "vetting," that you as a buyer may find very helpful. A vetted show means that a committee has gone through all the dealers' exhibits at this show and removed all reproductions and non-antiques.

One thing to remember when buying at an antiques show is that frequently the dealers are not from the area. It could be quite a costly and time-consuming business to find the dealer after the show closes. If you buy an early cast-iron mechanical bank, for example, receive a guarantee that it's original (always in writing and with the dealer's name on the receipt), and later find the bank is a reproduction, you could have a problem. The dealer might be on the road for a month or two. Try calling first and then sending a registered letter. Be prepared to wait. Usually the dealer will get back to you eventually and refund your money. Still, for some, the uncertainty is unsettling. If you have doubts, *any* doubts, about what you are buying, the rule is do not buy.

Photo by Moreton Marsh

5

Fakes, Reproductions, Restorations

D ISCERNING fakes, reproductions, and restorations gets into a no-man's land of claim and counterclaim. Even the most renowned experts have disagreed on what constitutes a fake and what is allowable restoration. This applies to furniture; accessories and anything else but furniture are another story.

Fakes are made to realize a profit for their seller, in almost every case. Note I said seller, not maker. There are well-substantiated cases of people turning out fine copies of genuine antiques and selling them for just what they are, low-priced copies of the genuine article. But at some point, someone realizes that either with just a little more work, or presented in the right setting to an unsuspecting buyer, the fakes will pass for the genuine piece and sell accordingly.

The reader must be aware that there lurks in the heart of the genuine antiques lover the urge to find the really great piece. It's akin to the Little Leaguer's dream of growing up to pitch a no-hitter in the World Series. We want the next item we buy to be that dynamite piece we've fantasized about. Sometimes this desire overwhelms our sense of reality. We forget all the rules we learned so arduously over the years. When we see that great piece tucked into a corner of the attic, we suspend our normal rules of caution. We believe the dealer who hauls the reproduction Windsor chair out of the back of his station wagon and proudly exclaims, "Look what I just picked up out of a house way back to hell-and-gone in the country!'' Understanding this search for the "Great Antique" helps explain why both dealers and collectors get stuck with the fakes.

Let's look at the furniture field. A reproduction is a piece made in the same style as a genuine antique, but not necessarily with the same woods, or in the same size, or with all the details of the original. A copy is a reproduction that is patterned exactly after an original piece. The majority of reproductions of American furniture were created after 1876. A lot of the furniture created by the larger furniture factories of this period has come to be known as Centennial. This doesn't imply that it was made for the Centennial. I've seen furniture made in the 1920s by the Grand Rapids factories called Centennial by auctioneers.

Remember this salient point: most, but not all, reproductions of early styles were made less than one hundred years ago. The tools used, the construction details, the finishes, the hardware, even the thickness of the wood used differ from those of the originals. No reputable antiques dealer will sell you a reproduction as a period piece. Once you've handled the original pieces, the differences become glaringly evident.

A copy of an original piece is a different story. Take the case of the celebrated Brewster chair purporting to be seventeenth century in origin that ended up on the cover of the Greenfield Village and Henry Ford Museum's pamphlet, "American Furniture 1620-1720." This great chair, supposedly two hundred and fifty years old, was the product of a living Rhode Island craftsman who painstakingly used elements of design of the original Pilgrim Century products, then aged the finished piece so successfully that it was accepted by the museum.

The maker of the chair kept two missing spindles and other remnants of the construction to validate his work. When these were produced, the museum x-rayed the chair and found that machine-made drill bits had been used in its construction. This discovery made national headlines in 1977 and woke up antiques collectors to the realization that fakes of this quality were indeed around.

But relax. Very few of these exist. The amount of time and labor required to produce them precludes any sizable number of them existing. Even the Brewster chair, had it entered the major auction route, would have had to eventually undergo severe scrutiny by the top experts in the furniture field. The reputable dealer who gets involved in the sale of a fake, almost always unknowingly, will buy back any piece he sold as original.

Realize that in order for it to be profitable to spend the time to produce a copy of a piece of antique furniture, the value of the finished product must be high. An average woodworker could turn out a copy of a late-eighteenth-century ladder-back chair. He could then spend several days painting it in a buttermilk red-based paint, then chipping the paint off, and sanding the wear points. Finally, he could apply a thin coat of varnish and bake the resultant finish to resemble age crazing. Then would come a new rush seat. He might even try to age the rush. For his labors he might realize the princely sum of $200. Worth it? Hardly.

Total fakes are rare but not unique. An experienced woodworker with a knowledge of the old techniques, a genuine piece to copy, and the ability to fake finishes can produce an amazing copy. Fortunately, most fakes get spotted. The antiques publications give wide coverage to these pieces.

What the average collector is apt to get stuck with is a restored piece or a piece with major replacements. Restoring means bringing back to original condition. If in the event of missing parts new parts are added, the piece has replacements. Major auction galleries will note in their catalogues if a piece is restored, or has replacements, although this is not an iron-clad rule. You may have to rely on your own knowledge to determine the degree of restoration.

For some auction houses restoration means simply regluing and refinishing. For others, restoration means the addition of missing pieces. Let the word "restoration" warn you that this piece has had work done to it. Actually you're better off with an auction house that notes restoration than one that doesn't, or with a dealer who notes the work on his offerings. Be aware that any piece that has had any work done on it is worth less than a piece in its original condition, providing the original condition is sound.

Frankly, over the years almost every piece of furniture has had some type of restoration. Let's face it, furniture was produced to be used. Our ancestors sat on chairs, slammed drawers, ate from tables, and slept on beds. Some pieces have had as little restoration as putting new screws in a sagging hinge, others had the glue blocks under the chair seat replaced. What bothers collectors and investors is the unreported restorations and replacements; the new lid on the fall-front desk, the replaced base on the chest of drawers.

Anyone with a knowledge of antique furniture can envision the base that would look proper on an eighteenth-century country chest of drawers. But then comes the problem for the restorer. If just a simple foot form would look nice, why not add an elaborate bracket cut-out form with scrolls, ears, and a deeply carved center rosette? If the restorer uses old wood and can fake the finish, he has possibly added as much as $2000 to the chest's basic value.

That kind of money makes unethical restorers listen. Any work on a piece that changes it into something it never was, that upgrades the whole object, is considered unethical in the eyes of reputable restorers. It is not illegal. That's an important thing to realize. If you buy a piece that has undergone major restoration and you are aware of it at the time of purchase, you own it and any resulting problems. Remember that most auction sales are as is and where is. A lot of dealers sell the same way.

Beyond restoration comes something that's not quite faking but is not just restoring either. Let's say I've picked up an early country tapered-leg drop-leaf table base in cherry. The remnant has never been painted and still has its old finish. I spot in a dealer's barn the top and both leaves from a cherry table. Well, obviously I'm going to get the two pieces together. Wait a minute, the top is too wide and the drops too long for my base. OK, I'll just narrow the top, cut down the leaves, form new rule joints, use old hinges, work on the finish, and I'll have a table to sell.

Up to this point all I have is a table with an old, but replaced, top. I haven't gone beyond the restorer who replaced a base to the chest of drawers. But let's see, I do have all that extra cherry on the table top to work with. What if I shape the table top, give it a gentle serpentine shape; that will make it into a country Pembroke or breakfast table. It will only take a few more hours of work. Wait a minute, I have a nice early small Hepplewhite drawer around here somewhere from a candle stand or lamp table. Here it is, and the drawer front is cherry. Now if I put that in one end ... See how it goes?

Yes it's a fake, and no it's not. The parts are all old. I only ask $600 from the first dealer and point out that the top is a replacement. Period. The top is a replacement. The dealer listens and nods. Two months later I see my table in another shop. The price is now $1500 and no one even mentions the word "replacement."

I call this kind of work reconstruction. You can call it what you want. It's a lot more prevalent than you think. I know restorers who work full time reconstructing furniture. It takes a lot of old parts and a lot of ability, but there are willing buyers for every finished piece. You have to be willing to get down on your knees to look over a piece. You have to know genuine antique furniture. You have to look for the new parts. Or, you have to trust your dealer.

The dilemma of refinished furniture also bothers a lot of collectors and dealers today. Let's face it, there was a time, in the 1940s, '50s, and '60s, when it seemed like everyone stripped their original finishes to see the "natural" wood color. There is an awful lot of very good furniture out there to be had that has absolutely nothing wrong with it, except that it doesn't have the original finish anymore.

Be aware that it is far easier to conceal major restoration by refinishing the entire piece than by any other method. When you are buying antique furniture with a totally new finish, pay extra attention and look for replacements. If you

97

have a piece of antique furniture that you are thinking of selling, get in touch with one of the major auction houses or a dealer and have them look at it in its original condition. It's worth more that way.

We find many shops that feature only refinished furniture. Why? Because many retail customers prefer their antique furniture to dovetail with their other, in-pristine-condition furniture. Fortunately for those who prefer their antiques to look new, there is a good bit of refinished furniture still around and there probably will continue to be.

I used to think that the one thing that couldn't be faked was an addition to or replacement on a piece of painted furniture. I knew about the wonderful buttermilk-based paints on the market that closely match the old colors, but to match perfectly just one area of a piece that has the old paint — well, that seemed unlikely.

But this last year I saw a tall pine-cased Grandfather clock in a dealer friend's shop. The grain-painted exterior was pure folk art. "Nice, isn't it?" she asked. "Well, look at this." She pointed a black, or ultraviolet, light at the top of the bonnet. Almost a third of the bonnet glowed eerily. After she switched the light off I examined the bonnet closely. The top third had been replaced and the paint matched perfectly.

She sighed. "I'm stuck with it. I have to tell people what it is." She's an honest dealer and I'm sure she did. It scared me though. No dealer wants to pass on a piece that isn't right. If we know that a piece isn't what it should be, we inform our buyer. The trouble comes when the seller doesn't tell the buyer.

Some dealers can recognize form through the finish and will take a chance on a good piece even if it is painted in 1920s white. We might do much turning upside down and looking inside with a flashlight to examine the construction of a heavily painted cupboard. We feel for the early plane marks and saw cuts, we look at the heads of the nails. Even then, there are those who won't buy incorrectly painted furniture.

Occasionally I find a wonderful piece of furniture but it is hidden under a hideous new coat of paint. Old paint I leave, usually, even if the color is apple green, but new (within twenty years) paint I usually strip, always by hand, trying to save the earlier finish.

I've even stripped the gloss polyurethane coat off a beauty of a little inlaid Federal candle stand, circa 1790. I had to tighten the glue joints on the piece and I wanted to see how it was constructed anyway, so stripping made sense. Once it was reglued and properly aligned, it received several coats of Minwax Hard Oil Finish. It sold as I was carrying it in the door of a very good antiques show to place in a dealer's booth. Yes, I did point out the refinishing.

I still don't know if the stripping is worth it though. About half the time I strip a piece, I find some major defect that doubles the work needed to make the piece salable. One time I stripped a mahogany drop-leaf table of early American Empire vintage, circa 1830. I found there was a reason for the black enamel covering the top: stripping revealed a 3/8-inch thickness of wood filler covering a massive flat-iron burn. I had to chisel away the former attempts to sand out the burn and inset a huge piece of mahogany into the opening. Two days later I sold the table and reckoned my labor at $20 a day.

Before leaving furniture and getting on to accessories, let's look at the ways you can protect yourself when faced with reproductions, copies, restorations, and replacements.

Reproductions: If you think you're being offered a reproduction instead of the real thing, the first step is to ascertain when the piece (assuming it's authentic) was made. If you are offered a Hepplewhite card table that was purportedly made between 1790 and 1810, there are several things to look for. First, does it *look* old? Stand back and look at it. Are there signs of wear? Even a refinished piece will show signs of age. Look underneath the table. Is there any evidence of the use of the hand tools of almost two hundred years ago? No book is a substitute for experience. The experts know what a real piece should look like. But even a novice knows that a nearly two hundred-year-old piece won't have circular-saw marks or the absolutely smooth feel a modern high-speed planer leaves on wood. Has the wood mellowed with age? Are you being given a hectic sales pitch? Is the price lower than it should be for a genuine piece? If so, back off.

Copies: Now you are up a grade. You can spot a reproduction from thirty feet, but this piece looks right. You check the form, you know the wood is consistent with that actually being used by cabinetmakers of the period. The finish seems old. What next? You look and feel for the evidence of the old tools used. You check for warpage of the wood. Wood shrinks across the grain. If it's tightly constricted, it has to crack. You look at legs. If they have aged over the years, they should not be perfectly round. You sight drawer fronts and sides looking for unevenness. You check for the patina that age leaves on wood. Finally, you look for that one thing that the fakers most often slip up on — wear. Remember though, wear without the evidence of age is no sure sign that a piece is genuine.

Restoration: If you consistently shop at an auction gallery that states "restored" in its catalogue, you probably know what this word means to it. For some, restored means the sanding or replaning of a table top that is severely scarred. For others, a new top. Expect that a restored chair usually means a chair with feet that have been replaced to bring it up to normal height. Look for lines or joints where new material has been added. Restored almost always means the finish has been replaced. Always check the drawer fronts to see if any new pieces of wood have been patched in to replace pieces broken off. Expect replacement hardware on any piece advertised as restored. Restoration is just another word for repairs. Look for signs of them.

Replacements: First, is any one thing glaring about the piece? Does the base seem a different color from the top? Is one leg better than the others? Can you see the line of a joint where no joint should be? Look inside, underneath, in back. Is one piece of wood a different color from the others? Does one area have a different feel than the rest? Are the nails or screws different in one area? One thing to consider that is common to both restoration and replacement is the smell of a piece. All strippers, glues, and finishes leave an odor that will linger for months on wood. This is especially true of a "case" piece — a piece that is essentially built as a case with doors or drawers in it. Try to get your head inside. Pull out a drawer, open the doors, and smell inside. Revealing, isn't it?

* * * * *

Once we leave the furniture field, the matter of reproductions and fakes grows much more simple. Simple in that the only reason for a reproduction's existence, according to some dealers, is to fool the buyer. A reproduction may start life as a low-priced copy of a scarce object, produced just to prove that the maker was capable of it; but once the piece exists, it's a sure bet that it will eventually be sold as the genuine object with the genuine object's price.

Many fakes — let's drop the word "reproductions" — are born the moment the collecting community discovers the desirability of an antique, and the resulting demand causes the prices to soar. As early as one hundred years ago, European porcelain factories had discovered that the demand for eighteenth-century porcelain from the finer makers had outstripped the supply. They obligingly solved this dilemma by faking the early products.

There is one prerequisite for the production of a fake: the original product must be valuable enough to warrant either the making of the mold or pattern or the hiring of the labor to turn out a hand-made object to afford the distributor a healthy profit. Thus it wasn't until the prices of the late-nineteenth-century cast-iron mechanical banks rose to a high level that the entrepreneurs invested in new molds, faked the older paint, and flooded the market.

Usually the life history of a mass-produced fake goes like this. The factory turns out a quantity. An enterprising buyer manages to acquire a number of the pieces before the general public is aware they exist. He ages the pieces by whatever method is needed: chipping and scuffing up paint, sanding the bottoms of glass pieces to simulate wear, burying them in manure or leaving them out in the rain to induce rust, or even heating them with a torch.

He then makes his rounds of the dealers, offering the pieces at fair wholesale prices. He might even sell one or two at the full retail price to a beginning collector. Sometimes he will sell five or six in the same town. He's got to move fast so he covers as much territory as he can. He may only have as little as two weeks to get rid of his stock.

Someone gets suspicious of this new supply of what was formerly a scarce item. Soon the word spreads. A national antiques magazine publicizes it. By the time the factory goes public with its line of reproductions, though, a last market remains for the hot shot. He hits the small auctions, the part-timers who don't read the big magazines. He sells to the little flea-market operators. By this time he's offering his stock at a fraction of his first-sale prices. People like bargains.

Another kind of faker is the one who is extremely knowledgeable about what is currently hot in the antiques market. This fellow knows what is rare. He keeps up with the auctions. He is either a craftsman himself or knows someone who is. He's not going to flood the market with a mass-produced item. He's going to be discerning about what he offers. And it's going to be extremely worthwhile monetarily.

In 1980 an interesting example of this type of fraud came to the attention of the antiques community. Back in 1978 a piece of American redware pottery sold at auction for a record price of $18,000. This piece, a small figure of a standing lion with its tail curved up onto its back and a flowing mane, was produced before 1880 by a Waynesboro, Pennsylvania, potter named John Bell. This fine example of pottery folk art had a well-documented family history. So did a few other similar examples that emerged shortly after the record sale.

By 1980 other lions had begun to surface. Then the news broke. A pottery in North Carolina was offering copies of the lion at prices ranging from $30 to $100. The pottery was not pretending that the lions, which were made of white clay instead of the red earthenware of the Bell lions, were anything but copies. Further research revealed that these copies had been sold to dealers and collectors for up to $5,000. The seller of the copies had skillfully applied the marks of age to his offerings.

Let it be added that, as always in an event like this, the dealers who were stung on the copies made restitution to their customers. But the point is, someone made a great profit as the first seller of a pretty good copy. Also something to remember is that the buyers in most cases had nothing to compare their purchases with. The few originals were so scarce that photographs were usually the only modes of comparison. When the copies were eventually placed side by side with an original, the differences were immediately evident.

As sure as God made little green apples, by the time this book reaches you there will be a new type of fake antique making the rounds. The ever-growing demand for quality antiques guarantees it. As a collector or investor, you must take certain steps to protect yourself. If you are buying from a dealer, you must ask for a signed, dated sales receipt stating that the object you are purchasing is original and giving a description of the object bought.

The large auction houses that issue catalogues of their sales also list their guarantees. Read them. Small auction houses vary in their guarantees. Some have none. *Caveat Emptor.* An expensive fake at a small auction could easily end up in the law courts.

Just be aware that any piece that purports to be a rare, expensive antique will bring a certain level of money. If you are offered this piece for considerably less, watch out. Take the time to do some research on similar pieces. Ask the experts.

To keep up on the current reproductions and fakes being sold as originals, read the antiques publications. If I could subscribe to only one publication today, it would be the *Maine Antique Digest.* This magazine, published in Waldoboro, Maine, by editor Samuel Pennington, is not as provincial as its name suggests. It covers the fakes, the national antiques shows, and the auctions, and tells what's going on in the business. It has produced many of the first reports on the "fake" market. Many dealers and pickers owe Sam Pennington a debt of gratitude and I hereby acknowledge mine.

It's interesting to think that the counter-culture movements of the 1960s and '70s may now give us future fake antiques. I went to a college that by 1970 offered courses in glass blowing, pottery, and metal working — all trades that could produce some wonderful copies of antiques. Indeed, the fakes offered in the last few years have included metal weather vanes, rare pieces of pottery, wrought-iron hardware, iron and tin lamps, fireplace equipment, and carved wooden decoys. I make it a point to visit crafts shows regularly to see what people are making.

Another type of fraud often encountered is the passing off of European antiques for American. European lighting devices are the most common example. Be aware that Spanish and other European lighting devices are far cheaper than American examples, and widely imported. Familiarize yourself with the American examples.

Frankly, as pertains to fakes, things are much healthier in the antiques market nowadays than they used to be. Collectors are more knowledgeable. We expose fakes as soon as we can. We publicize these fakes. The problem is that there is an amazing quantity of fakes in circulation that were produced during the last century.

For a description of the fakes recognized in former years, let's look at Ruth Webb Lee's book *Antique Fakes and Reproductions,* published in 1938. Just leafing through the illustrations, I note blown-glass pieces in American patterns, fake three-mold glass, Bohemian glass, pressed-glass pieces, historical flasks, reproduction Sandwich-glass lamps, hurricane shades and globes, hanging lamps, milk glass, dolphin candlesticks, paperweights, silver items, Staffordshire figures, fireplace fenders, and tin lanterns.

What's happened to those pieces, some of them old even then, but others produced just a few years prior to publication? Well, just a few weeks ago I stopped at a small shop in New Hampshire to view an amazing quantity of Bohemian glass. I'm certain I was looking at some of the pieces that Ruth Webb Lee had reported in 1938 were being imported in large quantities from Czechoslovakia. The lowest-priced piece I viewed was $40, and I know this particular dealer works on a very small markup.

Yes, the antiques business in most cases has assimilated the old fakes. Only when the price reaches the upper plateaus does anyone start to question the piece. Antique silver usually gets scrutinized. Other pieces work their way around from dealer to collector to dealer until they reach someone who questions them. Eventually they get back into the hands of a novice and off they go again.

Twelve years after Lee's book, Raymond F. Yates wrote *Antique Fakes and Their Detection* for Harper Brothers. Had things changed? Sadly, no. Yates added to Lee's list much furniture, a huge amount of Continental china, pewter, clocks, jewelry, silhouettes, primitive paintings, wax portraits, prints, and hardware. Now these pieces have been on the market for at least thirty years. Do they show up for sale? Yes.

A couple of years ago I attended an indoor show in Massachusetts, where I encountered small hollow-cut silhouettes in what seemed like every third dealer's booth. Finally there was one dealer with the same silhouettes for a price of $7 each, unframed. "They are new, of course," he explained. The cheapest one in the other dealers' booths was $40 framed and some were as high as $75. These weren't the same silhouettes reported by Yates in 1950, just a case of history repeating itself.

By this point maybe you think I'm guilty of overkill. Believe me, I'm not enjoying telling you that there are a number of fakes out there on the market. We dealers are policing ourselves. We don't want to sell fakes. More than that, we don't want to *buy* fakes. Besides hurting a dealer's reputation, it hurts his pocketbook when he has to buy them back from a customer. If every reproduction manufactured had to be clearly marked "reproduction," it would help. Sure, some entrepreneur would find a way to grind off or fill in the mark, but the very presence of the mark would help.

As long as it's in our natures to be greedy, we will continue to be unable to pass up a bargain. Most bargains on antiques are costly ones.

Oh, by the way, I buy reproductions. Why, you ask, after all this tirade about reproductions, would I buy them? I buy them for the same reason other dealers do — to use. A well-made reproduction piece of furniture is serviceable, fits in with antiques, and will last many years. If new kitchen chairs cost $150 each and antique Windsors $400 to $600 each, and I'm sitting at an auction that is letting reproductions go for $75 a piece — and I need kitchen chairs — what do you think I'm going to do? A lot of dealers furnish their houses with reproductions bought at auctions, especially auctions where no dealer cares to be seen buying a reproduction. Of course, we usually have someone else do the bidding for us. Pride, you know.

Courtesy of Patricia Anne Reed Antiques, Damariscotta, Me.

6

Accessories

THE beginning auction-goer is usually amazed at the array of antiques. He is confronted with table after table of things that he would never have believed there was a market for. As he sits through that first auction he is often astounded at the prices these items bring. There is literally a collector somewhere for everything. Barber poles? Don't scoff — early examples with old paint bring several hundred dollars. Pap boats? Never heard of them? "Pap boat" is another name for an invalid or infant feeder. These small-handled bowls have a spout to let the holder pour the contents directly into the invalid's mouth. They are found in a variety of shapes and materials. The most common are china or porcelain, but I've owned an eighteenth-century example in pewter. They too are collected.

You name it, from abacuses to xylophones, someone, somewhere, collects it. And it is going to eventually end up at an auction or in an antiques shop. That's what makes this business fun. Dealers and collectors are able to discern between the average item and the spectacular; that's why you see one piece bring $50 and what seems to be a similar piece climb as high as $150.

One mistake that a beginning collector makes is not buying the really choice examples from the very start. He concentrates instead on filling out his collection as quickly as possible, passing up expensive pieces because the same money will buy two or three lesser examples. Later when he does decide to add the great pieces to his collection, he finds that what he previously thought was expensive is now outrageous. Prices *are* going to rise. A beginning collector is advised to research the field before starting to collect; he should know the price ranges for the examples running from mediocre to best.

Then, if he is serious about the collection, he shouldn't pass up the finer items when the opportunity to buy them arises.

During the first few years I was in business, one collector in particular used to amaze me. This man would sit at auction after auction and outbid every dealer present for the really choice pieces of early iron. An average eighteenth-century whirling broiler would bring $30 to $40. Then a broiler with intricate wrought-iron work and a well-formed handle would come up. The auctioneer would ask jokingly for $50. Up would shoot this collector's hand. It didn't matter if someone bid against him. He'd just keep bidding. We watched him pay $100 at an auction where a similar but plain piece only brought $35. "Crazy!" we whispered. Crazy like a fox. Within a few years, the common pieces of iron were bringing the prices he'd paid for the best examples.

Eventually the collectors and dealers were routinely paying five to six times the prices this collector had paid, if they could find similar pieces. They usually couldn't.

*   *   *   *   *

Let's start with iron. The fireplace was the center of activity in the early-American home. Visit a museum or reconstructed country village, even look in the cook house at Mount Vernon, to see the wide array of implements used around the fireplace. From andirons and pokers, log turners and shovels, to pans, broilers, and toasters, iron was indispensable in an early kitchen.

Wallace Nutting's *Furniture Treasury* (Volumes 1 and 2 combined, Macmillan) is still the best place to see examples of the early pieces. It is also reasonably priced. All the early pieces were hand forged. Expect unevenness. Look for seams, where pieces were joined. The better examples will have that added bit of decoration that shows the maker cared for his product. Instead of a simple loop at the end of a shaft, the maker might have added an extra scroll. The broiler, with its revolving round grill, would have worked perfectly well with straight bars and would have been easier and quicker to make. But we find broilers made with serpentine bars. We see them with ornate scrolled ironwork. We find ladles with incised decoration. We see tall iron candle stands with brass ornamentation and round (penny) feet.

Expect any piece of iron used around fire to show the effects of fire. Look for warpage. Old iron will often be pitted. Door latches, hasps, and hinges will show wear from age and use. Do nothing to old iron but wash, dry, and apply a light coat of oil to it. Do not try to scrape away the signs of age. Above all, never use a wire brush on old iron. Don't try to make a piece of old iron shiny.

You may encounter an over-cleaned piece of old iron at an auction or in a shop. Over-cleaning will usually reduce the value of a piece drastically, sometimes fifty percent or more. Only an exceptional piece of iron retains its value after over-cleaning.

Museums have been among the worst culprits as far as over-cleaning goes. Many a museum collection sits there proudly in all its pristine, gleaming, over-cleaned condition evidencing not an iota of age. Few museums still over-clean today, but they can't change what has already been done.

If you are about to start collecting iron, become familiar with the original pieces. Read the books, visit the museums. Know what age looks like on iron. Why? Because iron is easy to reproduce. At most antiques shows I've visited in the last few years, I've run into at least one reproduction iron lighting device or fireplace implement being sold as old. A couple of years ago I walked out of a poorly-lit shop in Virginia having bought a very expensive rotating hanging bird spit that later proved to be new.

Under a bright light I was able to see where a rotary grinder had been used to smooth the arc-welded joints. In addition, I found a few of the little balls of metal created by arc welding, called spatter, that the maker had left. It was a good fake, but no piece of old iron should show signs of arc welding. The maker had used old pitted metal and had rubbed stove blacking over the piece to simulate age. I was lucky; the dealer refunded my money. She was stuck with a fake.

Today many European pieces are being sold as American

because they will then bring higher prices. The majority of these were produced relatively recently. I've seen French iron miners' lamps that were made in this century sold as antique.

*   *   *   *   *

One of the frustrations facing the collector of early brass and copper is that very few pieces were marked with the maker's name. We also know that the early colonists imported quantities of brass and copper items. The combination of these two facts makes it extremely difficult to positively identify American brass and copper items produced before the middle of the eighteenth century. Most of the brass and copper items found at auction or in the dealer's inventory are English or European if made before 1800.

Some American pieces were marked, though, and some of the marked pieces did have highly identifiable characteristics. By comparing an unmarked example with the marked piece we can often tell that the unmarked one is by the same maker. In fact, pieces from specific areas in America do show certain regional characteristics. We are able to look at a pair of brass andirons and determine, because of the shape of the top or the feet, that they were made in New England or New York.

I don't know of any current book in print that specializes in and accurately covers American brass or copper. I use a 1950 copy of *Early American Copper, Tin, and Brass* by Henry J. Kauffman (Medill McBride Co., New York) at my public library. Kauffman does include a listing of brass foundries and known coppersmiths and braziers working in America up to the early nineteenth century.

Candlesticks are highly collectible and easily identifiable by their shapes. Collectors use such specialized terms as "mid-drip" to describe their prizes. Good early (before 1700) candlesticks are not often encountered at a country auction or in the average dealer's shop. One of the reasons is that a seventeenth-century pair is worth the price of a new compact car. If you are interested in collecting early candlesticks, there is a good book to refer to: *Old Domestic Base-Metal*

Candlesticks by Ronald F. Michaelis (Antique Collectors Club, England, 1979), available from book dealers specializing in the antiques field.

Articles on brass and copper appear frequently in *The Magazine Antiques,* published monthly; and informative articles from this magazine have been compiled into an anthology, entitled *Antique Metalware: Brass, Copper, Bronze, Tin, Wrought and Cast Iron,* by Main Street publishers. It should be available at your book store. Main Street has brought out other anthologies of articles on accessories. They are quite good and moderately priced.

Besides candlesticks and andirons, what other articles are you apt to encounter? Dippers, ladles, and warming pans are the next items that turn up most frequently here in New England. Look for signed, or stamped, pieces. A maker's name on a piece of copper or brass can easily quadruple the value. Extra ornamentation on pieces does the same. Engraved decoration adds to the value.

Be aware that reproduction brass warming pans have been made for many years. Look for the signs of age and use. Push-up brass candlesticks are being reproduced too, and currently sell for under $20 a pair in New York City. Cast brass and buffed to a high luster, they are being offered without the push-ups. Considering that an old pair will retail for up to $200, depending on the shop and area, you know what's going to happen, don't you?

The undersides of the old ones have aged to a dark patina. But these copies are bright new brass. Old ones have nicks and scratches, new ones are pristine. Old ones have been polished so many times that their edges are slightly rounded. An old push-up will have an aged push-up rod, the cork or material filling the lower hole will be aged and worn.

Again, when you are buying brass and copper, look for evidence of age. Remember that these metals are relatively soft. They should have nicks, scratches, and sometimes dents. Any engraving should show wear from repeated polishing. If you insist on buying only pieces in pristine condition, you will probably end up with a reproduction.

For all our protestations, reproductions occupy a strange place in dealers' hearts. Yes, we hate them, especially when we watch customers buy them instead of our originals; but, yes again, they intrigue us when we see a particularly well-made copy and realize what we could do with it.

I've observed several well-known and reputable dealers pause when offered a great reproduction. Hell, I might as well admit it — I've succumbed to the temptation. Those dealers I've sold reproductions and fakes to have been informed of what they were buying, however.

We try to tip you off when you ask prices. You see three pieces in a row. Each piece has an average, fair price; then, a fourth piece causes us to pause, to cough slightly, to mention a price that is well below the industry-wide standard.

What do you think is happening? Why is that fourth piece cheap? If price is a consideration, if quality doesn't matter, we do have a piece for you — a reproduction.

* * * * *

A lot of people collect silver, and a lot more would like to. Silver can be found in most shops and seen at almost every auction. Let's go through a few facts about silver. The basic word used is "sterling." Around 1300 England ordained that silver objects had to be the same standard as the coinage. By law every piece of British silver had to be assayed by an appointed committee to make certain it contained the correct proportion of actual silver. To prove they had been assayed, they were stamped with a mark, called hallmark. British silver will have a minimum of three hallmarks and usually four or five.

After 1300, silver uses the sterling standard, which means that 925 parts out of 1000 are pure silver. The rest (75) are copper, or mostly copper. English and American silver up to the end of the Revolutionary War are of this standard or higher. The word "sterling" didn't come into common usage until after 1868 as a mark on American silver indicating that the silver conformed to the British standards.

The majority of silver sold in America is of British origin.

The collector of British silver can choose from among many books to research the hallmarks, and most public libraries will have at least one reliable volume. The use of date letters and individual town assay marks are so well regulated that most books are fairly similar in their research. I use *The Book of Old Silver: English, American, Foreign* by Seymour B. Wyler (Crown Publishers) for British and other foreign hallmarks.

The best book about American silver is *Early American Silver* by Martha Gandy Fales (Excalibur Books). She covers the styles found in America; the special features of American silver, fakes, and repairs. If you are about to collect American silver, her well-illustrated book is a must.

Identifying the makers' marks on American silver is a difficult job. There is no up-to-date book that positively identifies the marks of all the American makers. I use a book that lists fifteen hundred marks, *Marks of Early American Silversmiths* by Ernest M. Currier (R. A. Green). Although it is good as to the period it covers, new marks are found each year and the book therefore is not up to date. There is a monumental need for someone to correlate and verify all the known makers of silver in America.

The collector of later American silver may want to pick up a copy of *A Directory of American Silver, Pewter, and Silver Plate* by Ralph and Terry Kovel (Crown Publishers).

Good early American silver is still showing up at country auctions. Two years ago I saw a sugar shaker by Benjamin Burt (Boston, 1729-1805) slip through a Vermont auction for $125. This year I bought a 1783 Phi Beta Kappa key at auction for $35. It was similar to the ones shown in Fales' book. Silver is a specialized and usually expensive field. Quality examples of American silver would have bought a fine house just a few years ago and the best pieces will buy a country estate today.

The fakers have been aware of the value of silver for a long time. Pieces have been altered, added to, and engraved with old dates. Ignore the engraving on a piece of silver and pay attention to the form and maker. Someone might have wanted to honor his grandmother by presenting her with a silver pitcher with her birth date engraved on it. The date would be eighty years older than the pitcher. You must date the pitcher, not the engraving.

A faker will do even worse. Besides engraving a false date, he might add a lid from an old tankard to a jug, he might resolder an old hallmark to a newer piece. Sometimes the solder lines are visible. Heat will sometimes cause the repair to show up but don't expect to be able to conduct this test in a dealer's shop. It is best to buy expensive silver from an expert dealer.

The British have a very tough law about fakes. A piece of silver has to be marked accurately to the last component put on the piece. For example, if an 1870 cover is put on a 1750 tankard, the whole piece has to be marked 1870. If it isn't, the authorities confiscate the piece. We don't have any such law here. Our fake, or alteration, may be withdrawn from the auction block when an eagle-eyed collector complains, but once it is back into the hands of the consignor it is nobody's business what happens next. Usually it is resold.

There is some confusion among beginning collectors regarding silver-plated articles. The practice of fusing a sheet of copper with a layer of silver started in England, and the city that produced the majority of it is Sheffield. We now use that city's name to identify pieces made there between the years 1750 and 1838. After 1838 electroplating came into widespread use, and that created a problem because electroplated pieces are not what an experienced collector has in mind when he refers to Sheffield plate.

The pieces produced before 1820 are extremely collectable, and although prices aren't comparable to those of solid-silver pieces for the more common items, early Sheffield pieces of the best quality and by the rarest makers are nearly equal to the solid silver. Old Sheffield is often found with the copper showing through in worn spots. Don't have it replated. New silver never has the color of the old. Replating and/or repairing definitely lowers the value of old silver. Old Sheffield is often unmarked. When it is marked, it will have a maker's mark only and never a date letter.

We begin to see silver pieces marked with the maker's

name and the stamp "E.P." around the middle of the nineteenth century. "E.P." stands for electroplating. Later the initials "E.P.N.S." show up. They mean electroplated nickel silver. Obviously all items marked with either set of initials are much-lower-quality items than Sheffield plate.

One fact that has become evident in the past few years is that no one will ever again buy a piece of silver at auction for less than its melted value. Even at the most remote country auctions I hear the auctioneer call out the weight of a piece of silver he's offering. "How much does that pitcher weigh, boys?" One of the runners will reply, "Just over four ounces." The auctioneer will look sternly at the crowd. "You know what the price was just yesterday, don't you? Well, let's start it off for that and see where it goes."

The buyers with their scales are there at preview, weighing each piece and noting the weights in their notebooks. Some dealers and pickers have made handsome profits by letting the silver buyers get the pieces, then immediately offering them a profit. I saw a set of six coin-silver teaspoons sell for their weight value of $4 each and promptly be resold for $6. The next day they brought $20 each.

Selling your old silver for the silver content makes about as much sense as selling your old furniture for the firewood value.

* * * * *

Probably the most widely collected items in America are glass and china. Glass collecting, in all its forms, is probably enjoyed by the largest segment of the antiques community. Armed with price guides and collectors' handbooks, and lugging ponderous reference works, glass collectors can be found ranging far and wide in their efforts to widen their collections.

Just as there are different forms of glass — blown glass, pressed glass, cut glass — there are different forms to be collected within each category. Some people treasure bottles, others pressed cup plates.

Blown glass had been around long before the original Thirteen Colonies were even imagined. Historians have argued over several possible dates of its birth, but all we need care about is that it's several centuries old. And, as evidenced by today's examples, it's not about to pass away tomorrow.

Pressed glass came into production in America about 1825, although there were some experiments earlier. The same glass houses that had previously produced blown-glass merchandise evolved through blown-in-mold objects to the faster, more economical method of mechanically pressing the glass into molds or patterns.

Although some of the quality glass houses were decorating their finer pieces with engraving as early as the late eighteenth century, it wasn't until late in the first quarter of the nineteenth century that American cut glass appeared. The cutting of glass involves mechanically removing the surface of the blown or molded glass to give the object a totally new appearance and finish. The cut-glass piece is generally quite a bit heavier than the pressed piece, and is usually of heavily leaded crystal. It has to be, to survive the cutting procedure and still have enough substance left to be functional. The cut flats of the design reflect light differently from pressed glass. The cut edges are sharp, whereas pressed edges are not.

I give you all this information because I have seen many small operators trying to pass off pressed glass for cut glass on novice collectors. Before starting a collection, visit a reputable dealer and ask to see, touch, and hold a quality piece of cut glass. Ask first, because quality cut glass is very expensive and sometimes fragile. Taking a piece of cut glass from sunlight into a cold place will often cause it to crack. And putting it down too hard on a hard surface can cause chips. Be careful. Chips, flakes — any damage at all on a quality piece of glass — drastically reduce its price and salability.

Recently, many relatively new cut-glass pieces from Europe have been flooding America. Know your patterns if you collect glass. Most of these new pieces are not originally sold as antiques, but now and then one of them finds its way into a dealer's stock or comes up on the auction block. Even the older copies can fool a collector. Fifty years of wear can easily pass for one hundred fifty.

Reproductions are to be found in all forms of glassware. Blown- and pressed-glass reproductions have been around for decades, and most shops have been tricked at least once. I saw so much Mexican reproduction blown glass during my first year of dealing that I outsmarted myself.

I was once at an antiques show set in a beautiful New Hampshire town. The dealers were all quality dealers and had brought selections of their better stock. Perched on one dealer's table was a small, blue blown-glass pitcher with an applied handle. It had lovely form and shape. I picked it up to look at it as the dealer said, "It's Mexican, of course; it's only six dollars." The pitcher certainly looked authentic enough; coloration, applied circular foot and handle, even light scratches from wear on the bottom. It was a perfect copy of a typical South Jersey piece made prior to the nineteenth century. I put it down and passed on with the thought that there was an honest dealer.

In another section of the show I found an art-glass and early blown-glass specialist with her wares. I was still mulling over the small reproduction pitcher, so I decided to ask for a second opinion. The woman tending the booth said that the owner wasn't there just now; she was out looking at the other dealers' stock. I looked over her collection of early glass with the high, but fair, prices, and kept thinking of the blue pitcher. For only $6 it would be worth having as a reproduction. I'd just about decided to buy it when the dealer returned from her walk. And you guessed it — clutched safely in her hands was the blue pitcher.

"Even if I don't sell a piece of glass here," she proudly exclaimed, "it's all worth it. Look at this, a museum-quality South Jersey-type pitcher for only six dollars!"

"How much do you want for it?"

"Are you kidding? I'll never sell this; it's the only pitcher of its size I ever owned and I've had a lot of museum-quality glass in my day."

Later, looking through the great book *Two Hundred Years of American Blown Glass* by Helen and George S. McKearin (Bonanza Books), I decided she was right. The Mexican-reproduction description had unnerved me. But for only $6 it would have been a great shelf piece even if it was a reproduction. How much was this piece worth? Anywhere from $200 up.

The McKearins' other book, *American Glass* (Crown Publishers), with its three thousand-odd descriptions, charts, and tables of blown, molded, and pressed bottles, plates, flasks, vases, lamps, and candlesticks, is still the definitive book in the early-glass collecting field.

Objects manufactured in other countries for sale in America were subject to the McKinley Tariff Act passed in 1891 requiring imported objects to be marked with the country of origin. For example, a piece of pottery marked "England" was made after that date. Never mind that your teapot resembles a 1720 example in the reference book; if it is marked "Made in England" or simply "England," that's where it was made and it is newer than the year 1891.

Our import law of 1891 has been rather frustrated by foreign glass producers. Many a piece of glass has been shipped in labeled with the country of origin all right, but the information is on a paper label. Paper labels have a way of very handily coming off.

* * * * *

The broad name "ceramics" covers everything from the clay pottery being made in thousands of kilns today to the highly collected art pottery bringing thousands of dollars at the city auction galleries. The field can be roughly divided chronologically into four categories: earthenware, stoneware, porcelain, and art pottery. Remember that ceramics have always been imported into the United States. Excavations at early historical sites have produced quantities of imported objects and a minimum of American manufacture. I've dug at the site of a stagecoach stop in New Hampshire and found shards of English, French, German, and Chinese ceramics.

Of all foreign ceramics, those made in England are probably the most commonly found. Fortunately, they are usually well marked. The collector needs a general reference book, such as *The Encyclopedia of British Pottery and Porcelain Marks* by Geoffrey A. Godden (Bonanza Books), to aid him in his identifications. A large picture book such as *World Ceramics* by Robert J. Charleston (Chartwell Books) will help the beginning collector familiarize himself with various styles and forms from around the world.

Since ceramics have been produced for centuries and made in all countries, I'm only going to deal with those produced in America.

Earthenware is made from native clay, formed by hand or on a wheel, and fired at relatively low temperatures. The glaze is usually a simple lead glaze. Since the base clay was usually red, many collectors have come to call all this type of ceramics redware. The forms made range from everything used on the table to bean pots, jugs, whistles, and banks. Areas producing earthenware were normally all the Atlantic Coast states, New England, and later the Midwest. Antique earthenware is over one hundred years old. Remember, any competent potter can turn out a piece of earthenware. The pieces produced by a rural potter working two hundred years ago can be duplicated by a potter today. The genuine piece will have wear, sometimes even a repaired break.

To show how easily pottery can be duplicated, consider this. A friend recently showed me a small pottery figurine. Quite crude, unglazed, and very primitive in nature, it had all the feel and form of a native piece of art from some unspecified culture.

"Great, isn't it?" he asked. "Look at this." He handed over a yellowed letter from a large, well-known American museum. The letter was addressed to a New Hampshire resident and was dated in the 1920s. It attested to the fact that the piece of pottery owned by the New Hampshire resident was pre-Columbian in origin and very definitely of considerable, but unspecified, value.

We sat down and had a few beers. I couldn't keep my hands off the figurine. He knew I was going to come up with the question eventually. Finally I asked, "How much?"

He laughed. "I guess I'd better tell you. My eight year old

made that last week at school. They're showing them pottery in art class now, and when he came home with it, I remembered that letter. Had the damn thing for years. What do you think?"

Well, I was amazed. The letter was the icing on the cake. Outside of the few dealers consistently handling pre-Columbian pottery, I doubt many antiques dealers would have paused before buying the piece. Copies of early American pottery, if presented with a good story or what seems to be suitable documentation, could go the same route.

My friend put his figurine away in a drawer, folded up the letter, and smiled. "Sure would work, wouldn't it? Good thing I don't need the money right now."

To keep things in perspective, the highly decorated, incised, and painted antique Pennsylvania redware known as sgraffito is today worth the price of a new luxury car. This class of earthenware is best bought from a dealer who knows the field.

Stoneware is a relative newcomer to the ceramics field. First used in Germany, it made its way to America, via England, by the middle of the eighteenth century. It is nearly as hard as porcelain and is most familiar to the antiques collector in the form of jugs, crocks, pitchers, and other containers. Stoneware is usually grey in color. That which has been fired at a higher temperature or with different ingredients is called yellowware because of its color. The first stoneware products were simple containers. Later, colored glazes were used and the forms were extended to encompass many of the products being produced in porcelain.

The containers were often given a simple decoration in blue, brown, or ocher. From the first splashes of color, decorations evolved into full pictures of birds, fish, deer, and even people. Decorated stoneware has grown into a highly collectable field today, the best selling for thousands of dollars.

Years ago collectors wouldn't buy any examples with damage, but today people will purchase pieces with chips, flakes, and even some cracks, depending on the extent of the damage. Avoid stoneware that has a crack running completely around the piece or through the decoration. Also avoid a badly flaking piece.

By the mid nineteenth century American manufacturers were turning out spittoons, pitchers, teapots, figurines, and other products with what is known as a Rockingham glaze. This mottled brown-and-yellow glaze was copied from the English and is not in itself evidence of American manufacture. Bennington, Vermont, did turn out many Rockingham products, as did most American potteries.

"Porcelain" is another word for china, the plates you eat from. China was an appropriate name for it, that country having made the first examples of porcelain, in the ninth century. Almost all the porcelain used in this country before 1826 was imported. I say "almost all" because although there were a few scattered attempts at producing porcelain, very few examples survived. The first factory with any number of surviving wares was the Tucker factory in Philadelphia. Tucker pieces were classical in form. Indeed, from 1826 on, most American porcelain was decidedly European in form, with classic shapes and decorations.

Factories from New York to the Midwest began producing porcelain around the middle of the nineteenth century. Because it had taken so many years to successfully develop the techniques involved, American porcelain manufacturers found it nearly impossible to compete with other countries. The European products were cheap and plentiful, and there was status in owning them. If you couldn't compete in the market for the common tableware, what could you do? Well, you could produce the next class of ceramics.

Art pottery began to appear on the scene about 1876 and was a logical consequence of the Arts and Crafts Movement. Art pottery is a controversial subject among some antiques buffs. Most of the pieces don't strictly qualify as antiques since they aren't one hundred years old yet. Neither is the furniture of the Arts and Crafts Movement, but both are avidly collected. People have been arguing for years about when style died in America. The late Wallace Nutting, author and collector, maintained that there was no style in America after 1830.

Many agree with him. Our late American Empire and Victorian furniture certainly borrowed freely from every prior style that ever existed.

The Arts-and-Crafts-Movement style was an "event" in the hodgepodge of existing design. Furniture of the movement threw out the superfluous excess of turnings and curves and went right to the bare necessity of lines and angles. Form was function. The minimum was enough. The sparseness was almost Oriental in nature.

Pottery started the trend. The earliest pieces showed their Victorian ancestry, but within a few years form and decoration began to leave behind any pretense of the rococo. Shapes were new to the eye; some were even primitive in their starkness. Glazes were allowed to run or drip. They became part of the form. The pottery known as Dedham had a crackled glaze. Decorations were minimal, often Oriental or evocative of American Indian. Underglaze colors were rich, glazes seemed translucent.

What factories made the wares? Among others we find Rookwood, Van Briggle, Dedham, Grueby, Weller, George Ohr, and Tiffany. Once you've seen a few examples of art pottery, you will recognize it. It began to die out after the First World War. Only a few factories producing it were left by 1930. Lest you think it foolish to even write about something as new as art pottery, consider this. In 1980 a piece of Rookwood pottery with an Indian chief as decoration brought $32,000 at auction.

A very good reference book for American ceramics is *The Pottery and Porcelain of the United States and Marks of American Potters* by Edwin A. Barber (published by Feingold & Lewis, distributed by J. & J. Publishing). It is a 1976 reprint of Barber's 1909 third revised edition, but there isn't much else on the market to compare with it. The writing is dated, but for information on potters and marks, it's invaluable.

One small volume by Marvin D. Schwartz, *Collectors' Guide to Antique American Ceramics* (Doubleday), gives the reader a clear understanding of this field. It is illustrated.

Before leaving ceramics, a word is in order about condition. Most collectors prefer to leave any damage — chips, flakes, etc. There are people today who advertise expert repair of ceramics. If you are considering ever selling any of your treasures, I advise you not to have them repaired. Some buyers insist on examining a potential purchase under a black, or ultraviolet, light, under which the repair will show up. Collectors would rather see the damage.

If you are not considering selling the piece and you've just busted Grandma Jones' Sèvres teapot, then by all means have it repaired. The better firms can do some amazing work. Often the collector will encounter a piece with old repairs. A broken piece will have been rejoined with metal staples. An expert can actually date the repair by the type of staples used and the method of repairing. Leave this repair alone.

Considering the use and abuse ceramics were subjected to, it's a wonder that as many pieces survived unscathed as did. Some collectors, who used to pass up any piece that showed damage, are now buying the rarer pieces in any condition. Still, one rule is unchanged: a perfect example is worth more than a damaged one, if it is authentic.

*   *   *   *   *

A term often encountered today is "folk art." Folk art has been appreciated and collected for years by a few of the pioneer collectors, but the general public was made aware of the term by the stunning show first mounted at the Whitney Museum of American Art, in New York City, in 1974.

To review that show and see what constitutes folk art, read *The Flowering of American Folk Art, 1776-1876* by Jean Lipman and Alice Winchester (The Viking Press). There are varying definitions of the term but I interpret "American folk art" as the art of the nonacademic artists of America working in any medium and expressing their feelings for decoration, scale, and form. It's a hard term to pin down. A painting doesn't have to be naive or crude to be folk art, although it may be. A painting by a well-trained artist doing an academic rendering of a subject in a formal manner is not folk art. Folk art is generally just that — the art of the common folks not following the well-established standards of the time but depicting their own views or using their own standards of decoration.

Obviously, paintings fit the definition. So do samplers, other needlework pictures, sculpture, non-factory-made toys, signs, kitchen implements made by craftsmen who brought that extra bit of decoration or art to the form, furniture that either left the traditional form or was decorated in a non-traditional style, quilts, and decorated stoneware.

One of the few mass-produced forms to be accepted as folk art is the weather vane. Individually hand-made weather vanes certainly qualify as folk art but the majority found on the market were made in factories. Nearly every barn or public building in America sported a weather vane at one time. Because of the size and availability of weather vanes, they have become much desired by the folk-art collector. Currently, the top price paid for a weather vane stands at $50,000. That's a private, not auction, price, for a carved wooden vane.

Just the fact that a piece of folk art is expensive is no guarantee that it is genuine, however. Folk art is a field that lends itself easily to exploitation by a faker. Reproduction weather vanes are not a new phenomenon. What is new is the artificial aging showing on the reproductions. This usually takes the form of a grey-green colored chemical that attempts to duplicate patina.

Ten years ago I was fooled on the first weather vane I saw. I bought it and resold it, and no one, including me, was the wiser. Within a few weeks others began to appear. By the time they were recognized as copies, my buyer had resold his and it had traveled way out of the area. I've been watching them make their way into the auction arena sporadically ever since. It didn't seem like anybody would have the guts to peddle them today.

Recently I visited a shop and the owner pointed out the horse-and-sulky weather vane she'd bought from a picker. She trusted her picker but he'd sold her a fake. If you are buying weather vanes, or any other form of folk art, you must see the originals for comparison.

Folk art is one of the trickiest areas to write about because it involves taste. It certainly confirms the axiom about beauty being in the eye of the beholder. I love folk art. I've bought and sold it for years. New England has produced some amazing pieces. I have been lucky, my buyers have shared my eye for the form or my feeling for the piece.

I am a bit upset about the pieces being sold today under the label "folk art." Folk art should have that little bit of something extra that carries the piece into the art range. A piece of decorated furniture should have more than the simple grained painting used by the area's craftsmen. The painter must have expressed his individuality with the medium. A Pennsylvania birth record should be painted by an individual, not printed by a job-press shop. The quilt should deviate from similar examples found in the area and show the individual character of the maker.

What constitutes art is too large a subject to go into here. What is certain is that folk art is hot today and brings large amounts of money when sold. A lot of merchandise is being offered under the name. You have to decide what folk art means to you. I think you should buy pieces that are individually created, and that evidence a personality. They won't be cheap. After all, you're buying art, and art is never cheap.

*　*　*　*　*

I've only scratched the surface but I've tried to give you, in discussing just these few fields, an understanding of the steps you should go through to successfully collect anything. What holds true for iron, brass, silver, or glass holds true for tools, prints, quilts, or antique umbrellas. Read every book on the subject in which you're interested, visit the museums, haunt the shops, attend the auction previews, talk to the dealers, find out who else collects, know what the price ranges are, be able to spot the fakes, and *then* start your collection.

Courtesy of Guyette's Antiques, Farmington, Me.

7

Investing
and Collecting

THERE are those who have watched the rapid price increases of antiques in the last decade and thought, "Boy, did I miss the boat by not investing in antiques! If I'd only owned that set of chairs that just sold for $180,000. I heard the owner bought them less than ten years ago for under $20,000." It is true, antiques have skyrocketed in demand and price, but in most cases the prices you see so publicized are for pieces owned by collectors, not investors. What's the difference?

Perhaps the difference is found in the similarity. Collectors and investors try to buy pieces that won't lose money when their collections are eventually sold. They avoid fakes and reproductions. They know that a well-put-together collection should increase in value. But now the difference enters. A collector likes, maybe even loves, the objects he collects. The investor has bought to realize a profit, period. No one likes to lose money, but the collector can discount the loss if the collection does finally sell for less than he's paid by considering the amount of enjoyment that building and having the collection has brought him. The investor can just chalk it up to a bad investment.

Collectors expect to study their fields, they spend time at collecting. An investor often just wants to invest money.

The basic point to investing is to buy an antique, own it for a specific amount of time, and sell it for enough money to cover the cost of having kept it but still realize a profit. If the profit doesn't figure out to be as much a year as you could have made on another investment, then the antique could be

129

termed a bad investment.

What are the costs of investing in antiques? First, there are initial purchase prices; if you bought at an auction that uses a ten-percent buyer's premium, that has to be included. Then there is maintenance and housing for the antiques for the period of time you own them. Plus insurance against fire and theft.

But there is yet another cost that many people who contemplate investing in antiques neglect to consider. How will you eventually sell your antiques and how much might that cost you?

If you put them into the auction arena, there will be a ten- to twenty-percent commission to be figured on. Some auction houses will charge you for insurance, photographs, and/or handling.

If you sell to a dealer, you must decide on a price that will be reasonable. Should three or four big dealers turn down your offerings, don't think they will keep quiet about it if you drop the same pieces into an auction.

If you choose to sell to another collector, how are you going to find him? The dealers buying for collectors at the big auctions certainly aren't passing their names around like candy.

As you can see, investing in antiques isn't as simple as putting your money into a money-market fund or buying a certificate of deposit. *The money you invest in antiques is in almost all cases not quickly convertible into cash.* If you do have a need to quickly unload your antiques, there is always a dealer or auction house somewhere that will purchase them, but you can expect a substantial loss, or at the very least to barely break even.

Remember, too, that if you do sell your investment antiques at auction, you have no control over the prices they will bring. You can set a minimum bid, or reserve, but if the reserve is too high and a piece has to be "bought in" by the house (no legitimate bid above the reserve figure), the house may well charge you a minimum commission for handling it in addition to the other fees. If a piece doesn't sell at that first auction, it has drastically hurt its chances of selling at those prices later.

It is very important that a piece offered at auction makes its reserve. The day in, day out population at the auction galleries is largely composed of dealers and a few collectors. It's a pretty tightly knit community and, although there may be competitors, the lines of communication are open. A piece that fails to make its reserve at one auction will be noticed and discussed when it reappears at another.

Many dealers feel that it is far better to err on the underside of a reserve estimate than to be high. But now comes the tough part. Are you, as an investor with $20,000 tied up in a piece of furniture, willing to see it listed with an $18,000 reserve? If the piece takes off and climbs to $30,000, you won't cry over where it started; but if it starts at $15,000 and only goes to $18,500, I know I'm going to see some tears, especially when you consider the commission and other costs.

I'm going to give one cardinal rule for investing. *An investor has to think and act like a collector or he shouldn't be investing in antiques.* This means you study the field before buying; you are familiar with form; you are able to recognize the bad, the mediocre, the good, and the best. You talk with the experts; you go to the auctions and examine the merchandise; you listen and read so that you know what is being faked, what isn't selling and why.

So relax. If you prepare yourself in this way, you're in pretty good shape. Your investments are fairly secure. Maybe I should say "your collection" because that is really what it is.

You can go back to the dealers you bought from and perhaps make a profit if enough time has passed. Your pieces should bring more at auction now, too. You didn't buy copies, fakes, or heavily restored pieces at outrageous prices to start with. You didn't get carried away with the bidding and battle another investor all the way up to twice the value of a piece.

Even considering that you did all the right things before spending your first cent on antiques, it is still possible to lose money when selling. Why? That comes from the very nature of a free-market economy. When the demand is high the prices will follow. At the time of this writing, the demand is high for good examples of period American furniture. The prices are very strong and expected to stay that way into the immediate future. If the demand slacks off or goes to another field, the prices will stabilize or drop.

Take a hypothetical situation. You decide to invest in the circa 1900 furniture of the Arts and Crafts Movement. You've done your research, talked to the experts, checked out the prevailing prices. It's a relatively new market and not many auction records on it are available. You attend an auction and spend $10,000 for five pieces. Three years later you decide to unload. You find a competent auction house that will advertise your pieces. Yours are not the only examples of that type in the auction. The auction house pulls in several more pieces from other consignors. Everything looks OK.

Disaster. Pieces barely make their minimums, some of the other consignors' stock doesn't even make the reserves. What happened? You find out later that all the new smart money is going out of furniture and into art pottery, just the reverse of what was happening when you were buying. (If you are investing in Arts and Crafts Movement furniture, don't rush out and sell your pieces because of what I've written; this is only an example!)

A multitude of events can affect the auction prices your investment antique could bring. Another important auction or antiques show being held on the same date as the auction your pieces are in could affect attendance and bidding. Your pieces being in an auction with mediocre offerings could affect the prices. A question or controversy about your pieces could hurt bidding. If you bought a piece at auction and later the question was raised about the validity of that first auction description, it could strongly affect the price the piece would bring at a later auction.

Having second thoughts about investing in antiques? Maybe you should. I know you should if you think investing means just picking a field, buying to your limit, waiting five years, and selling. If you have come to view investing as collecting, with an eye toward making a profit when the collection is sold, you are on the right track. There is only one *sure* way to invest in antiques. That is to hold a piece bought at a reasonable price until the price of all similar pieces is enough above what you paid to permit you to deduct the costs of buying, keeping, and selling your piece and still make a profit.

Let's take an example. Last year you bought a Tiffany table lamp in the Arabian pattern. You bought it at auction and paid $3500 for it, plus a ten-percent buyer's commission. You keep it at home in the library and have added it to the homeowner's insurance policy you already had in force. You determine it costs under $50 a year to insure and house.

If you are figuring on that lamp as an investment, it will have to bring at least $4350 at auction for you to make a measly $15 profit a year later ($3500 initial price, plus $350 buyer's commission, plus $50 insurance and handling, plus $435 seller's commission on a $4350 sale). If, when you check out the area auction prices, no Tiffany lamp of similar type is bringing that price, you can't sell.

You can safely consign your investment to auction only when those average sales figures for similar pieces are above your costs. Note I said "safely." Many will take a chance, and it *is* a chance. Just possibly your lamp might attract spirited bidding and soar to $6000. It's possible. The safe investor will not take the chance.

(That probably explains why most of the record prices set at auction are paid by dealers, or dealers bidding for museums. Dealers will buy for stock, knowing that they control the markup. What dealers will pay helps establish the price levels for a specific form. Dealers will often pay far over a previously established price because they recognize the potential of a piece. It's a brave soul or a foolhardy individual who will outbid a dealer and set a new price record for a piece. Take your pick.)

Even if you bought at a reasonable level and waited to sell until you were sure that your pieces were going to make you a profit, can you call antiques a good investment? Have you considered what your money would earn invested in another form? Do you have a fixed amount to invest that has to bring you a certain rate of return? Do you need an absolutely safe investment? Is liquidity a problem for you, or could it be?

Depending on your answers to these questions, investing in antiques might not make sense for you. However, a collection of antiques, carefully chosen and enjoyed while owned, may make a lot of sense and could even return you a nice profit when it is eventually sold. Consider it an investment then, if you wish, but not an investment that carries with it your life's success or failure.

If you are determined to invest in antiques, and it is to be strictly an investment — not a collection for enjoyment but a money-making proposition — there is one thing you must do. See a tax lawyer and find out what the IRS regulations are pertaining to investments. They change, and there are new rulings periodically. You are going to need that lawyer.

Having done all I can do to discourage you from viewing antiques as an easy in, easy out investment, let me proceed with a list of investment antiques and techniques. Remember, I recommend these antiques in the framework of building a collection with a potential, not guaranteed, profit. I'm using this criterion throughout this chapter.

An investor with under $1000 a year to invest is at both a disadvantage and an advantage. He can't compete with the moneyed crowd at auctions who can buy whatever pleases them, but he can specialize and still manage to put together a nice collection.

Let me give you an example. A friend of mine and his wife decided to put together a collection of antique salt dishes and spoons. They now have over three hundred examples proudly displayed in built-in glass cases in their dining room. The pieces are small, they don't take up a lot of room. The top price they've paid is just under $50 for a piece. Most ran around the $10 to $20 range. They manage to pick up at least one piece at every antiques show they attend. Sometimes they run into another collector, but in general there isn't much competition. At auctions they compete with a few dealers but since they are willing to pay up to a retail price for what they want, they usually end up paying over wholesale but not a full retail price, and walking out with what they bid on.

They have chosen a field to invest in, one that is not a hot mover in the shops. There are no sensationally high prices in the field being recorded in the antiques journals. They simply enjoy the hunt. One single salt dish doesn't look impressive. Several hundred, classed as to type and age, do. As the collection gets larger and more impressive the value does rise. This is the type of collection an investor with under $1000 a year does best at.

Consider other antiques that could work as well. Tools, for example. A collection of woodworking tools could be built for under $1000. It's a little more difficult now than it was two years ago but it can still be done. Although the rare signed molding planes may reach $600 to $700, there are many others to be had for under $50. The collector/investor will have to research the field, choose carefully, and live with his limits, but he can still put together a collection that should increase in value.

How about the ceramics field? Art pottery is high now and the demand is intense, but how about the pieces produced by the American factories during their difficult period of 1850 to 1900? I could put together a collection of pieces produced by the Bennington factory during this period for less than $1000 a year and have an impressive collection within three years. I might have to pass up some of the decorated stoneware that is collected as folk art but except for those pieces it would be a very nice collection. Maybe I'd concentrate on filling out the collection with a couple of purchases, using my entire year's allowance.

It would be hard to build an impressive collection of furniture for under $1000 a year, but you could certainly do it in the fields of glass, paper, woodenware, and tin, to name a few. The main criterion has to be that the object must be available and not yet priced out of reach. Collections that show the biggest increase in value were put together before the general collecting population was widely collecting them.

Even a collection of ordinary utilitarian objects should increase in value because of the fact that it is a collection. One piece is worth a certain price. A collection of objects increases the value of the single object within it. But there are exceptions to this rule. Fifty wooden potato mashers are probably going to flood the market and equal out to less than the price of one offered alone if they are all more or less of the same type and quality. But if each is of a different wood, type, quality, and decoration, it's a different story. The collection must be carefully chosen. The investor must study the field and use good judgment.

The advantage of forming a collection, even for under $1000 a year, is that it permits the investor to average out his investment: he may have made a mistake in the early part of his collecting career by spending too much on the first examples; now that he has added other pieces he can average his costs. When and if he finally sells his collection, the price realized can be averaged also. The early mistakes won't seem as important then.

Even this small investor can take advantage of the methods used by the large investor. He can place his collection on display at the local historical society or library. He can loan the collection to as many public places as possible. He can invest in producing a booklet describing the collection. If he can afford to, he can have the collection photographed and included in the booklet. What he is trying to do is establish something called "provenance" for his collection: he wants the public to associate the collection with his name. He is building up a reputation for the collection. At this juncture let me point out that for this to work, the collection has to be truly impressive and well put together, and not just an average grouping.

The investor should include the unusual, the rare, and the unique pieces among his collection. These won't be inexpensive, so he must be willing to pay double and triple the price of the average piece for them. He can't afford to ignore them though; they are what establishes the desirability of his collection. Always be on the lookout for the unusual examples. They separate the great collection from the average.

When he is ready to sell the collection, he has to choose

an auctioneer with care. He stresses the provenance: it is the "John Doe Collection"; the places it has been shown are named and the pieces are listed with their catalogue or booklet numbers. It usually works. The prices paid are much higher than those paid for anonymous pieces.

There is another approach the small investor can use, although it's not an approach for everyone. In addition to acting like the collector, the investor must also act like the dealer. He must not only *study* the field, he must *know* it. He is going to sink his whole investment into one piece each year. He has researched his field, be it furniture or silver; he knows the price ranges; he has watched the growth of an object's price over the years. Now he watches the auctions, he visits the shops. When he finds a piece that he feels has this potential for steady appreciation, he buys it. He watches the market. Each year he buys another piece. When he feels the market for his purchase has peaked, he sells and reinvests.

I say this approach isn't for everyone because the average antiques buyer is not willing to put forth the effort required to make this approach work. If you only have $1000 a year to invest in antiques and you aren't that sure about your knowledge, you're better off building a collection and sticking to what you do know.

An investor with up to $10,000 a year to invest in antiques is in a good position for putting together a collection but if he is trying to collect furniture, he too will find there are limitations. A lot of the furniture made before the Federal period is out of reach for the $10,000 investor. He can buy some pieces, but to form a true period collection will be difficult, if not impossible. What he *can* do is put together a room of Hepplewhite or Sheraton furniture, or buy a number of examples of American Empire or Victorian furniture.

But just a collection of furniture isn't enough to be called an investment. You want it to appreciate. The furniture offered at any auction hall could be grouped into settings or collections, and often is. You want yours to be better than average. Why not specialize? How about concentrating on all-cherry pieces? Or an American Empire dining room with every mahogany piece featuring bird's-eye maple veneer inlays? Live in Maine? Put together a collection of Maine-made pieces.

What you are trying to do is make your collection unique. There are a lot of collections of American furniture but how about a collection of only American children's furniture? Once you get away from formal period furniture, there are a lot of possibilities. Country furniture offers a wide variety to choose from. You could put together an entire kitchen of only old yellow-painted pine furniture. You could look for only stencil-decorated furniture.

In Victorian-era furniture you also have a chance to specialize. The prices being paid for Rococo Revival pieces made by craftsmen like John Henry Belter are extremely high now. How about assembling pieces from the Louis XVI Revival, which flourished from 1860 to 1880? Remember that you are always trying to make your collection special. Find a unifying point around which to build your collection.

A fine silver collection can be built for under $10,000 a year. You could specialize in a form, an area, or a single silversmith. For that money you probably wouldn't be collecting a lot of colonial silver but you could handle nineteenth-century examples.

You could build a small collection of samplers, a nice assortment of quilts or hooked rugs, a good tool collection, a modest folk-art grouping, etc. The one thing you will want to make sure of is that you don't include reproductions, fakes, poor-quality examples, or heavily restored pieces in your collection. Good pieces will always be in demand. The lesser examples may increase in value but only after the prices of all the rest have climbed, and never to the same extent.

If you decide to shoot the whole works on just one piece a year, you'd better be very certain of your knowledge. It's a funny thing, but I think the person with the smaller amount to invest is probably the more careful buyer — he can't afford to blow his whole roll on a mistake, so, if anything, he's overly cautious. The one with $10,000, by contrast, is apt to buy the married highboy, the chest on frame with the restored base, the card table with the wrong top, that sort of thing; he is in the price range where the not-quite-right pieces show up.

Unless you have done your homework and know what to look for when you are buying at auction, I'd advise you to buy from a dealer. The better furniture dealers will give you a guarantee for the piece you're buying. Some will even offer a buy-back policy for the future. Wait a minute, you say; I want to make money on this piece, I don't want just to sell it back for a small profit.

Well, are you good enough to sit out there in the crowd at the auction hall and compete against those dealers? Do you trust yourself to pay up to $10,000 for a piece at auction? If the answer is no to either of those questions, you should buy from the dealer. If you buy a good piece from a dealer, he may come to you in a few years and try to buy the piece back for a substantial profit. There is no guarantee about that, of course, but remember what you are trying to do. You are trying to buy a piece that is still reasonably priced and one you expect to increase in value in the future.

We are not talking about simply buying an antique for use. We are talking about purchasing an antique, or building a collection of antiques with the purpose of making a profit when they are sold. You may make a profit on those functional antiques when you replace them, but you may not. If you are serious about investing, you have to out-think other investors. Either you assemble a collection that increases in value because of your skill and taste in the assembling, or you anticipate the future demand for the objects you collect.

There isn't any other way. An investor might get lucky with the scatter-shot approach of buying, but usually that's all it is, just luck. Some people are lucky. You've seen what the economics of investing are. If you hope to beat those costs, keep up with inflation, and make a better profit than you could in a more secure market, you have to obey the rules.

With your $10,000 capital you can put together a collection within a few years that you can really hype if you choose to do so. When you send your collection out on loan, you can put up some extra money and have a professional pamphlet or booklet printed with color pictures. However, if the quality of your collection isn't up to par, no amount of hype will help it.

The majority of dealers, collectors, and investors are perceptive people. They know what you are doing. If you try selling a mediocre or average collection as the best thing to come down the pike since sliced bread, you're in for an awful shock. On the other hand, if the collection is above average and well put together, it will show up in gross sales figures.

Oh, to be in the position to never have to worry about money! To be able to invest in any antique one wanted to with absolutely no limits. It's a fantasy that most dealers have had at some time in their lives. Although it's only a dream for most of us, there are a few for whom it's a reality. Do you think that money is the prime ingredient in building an antiques collection? I'm not knocking its importance, you can't buy without it. But money isn't enough, not by itself surely!

There have been great collections sold on the collectors' deaths, and over the years many of these premier collections, assembled without regard to cost, have been found to contain more than just a small percentage of fakes, heavily restored pieces, and pieces of doubtful ancestry. No, money isn't enough. The collector must have expertise. Mix the expertise with capital and you have the recipe for a truly great collection. A truly great collection is a good investment.

The few readers who find themselves in the position of having both unlimited funds and true expertise in antiques are lucky. They know whom they are competing against at auctions — the private museum buyers, the top ten percent of antiques dealers, and a few other private buyers like themselves. It's an elite gathering up there. One thing is for certain, when you are paying over $100,000 for a piece, be it furniture or silver, you're not buying to throw it back into the auction arena in a few years.

The million-dollar painting belongs in the same category. Investors in this category are forming or adding to a collection. They're building estates. No one pays $225,000 for a piece of furniture hoping for a fast-buck profit in two years. These investors know that quality antiques appreciate over a period of years, just as the oil-company stocks in their portfolios do. In most cases these collections will stay intact until their collectors' deaths.

These are the people who buy from the dealers who make the headlines by paying record prices. They wait to see what the dealers will pay and then buy the pieces from the dealers. In some cases they will pay the dealer to go to the auction, look the piece over, make the decision, and buy the piece. At this price level they don't want to take the chance of making a mistake. They trust the dealer.

Knowing you can live with a piece for the rest of your life takes a lot of the edge off of investing in antiques. You don't have to give a piece a pedigree, it came with one when you bought it. You don't need to hype a piece, the national magazines very politely ask you to please let them photograph your collection. Authors doing research ask you for the opportunity to include your chairs in the books they're doing. And when finally the collection is sold, your name is firmly fixed in all the future provenance for the pieces. Oh, it is different at the top.

Within the last couple of years another type of antiques-investment plan has developed. This is the limited-partnership method of investment. What it is in the simplest form is a group of investors pooling their money to buy antiques for investment under the direction of the company head. The individual partners have no say about what objects are purchased. The antiques are usually loaned to museums immediately upon purchase. All costs of operation come out of the company fund. The partnerships are for a fixed period and are often non-transferable.

This type of investment plan appeals to those who don't want the bother of actually owning antiques, have the necessary capital (a limited-partnership share is not cheap), are willing to trust the judgment of the director of the plan, and believe in the future growth of antiques values. It is the counterpart of the stock market's mutual funds.

There are drawbacks to this type of fund. The key to successful investing is the purchases made. All the purchasing power is vested in the plan's head. If this person is knowledgeable, astute, and wise, all is fine. If not, well. . . . There are also the museums' positions to consider. More and more museums are becoming unwilling to accept objects for a limited number of years knowing that they will be sold with their names attached for provenance. In addition to both these drawbacks, there is one other reason the limited-partnership plan doesn't appeal to some: it's too remote. The fun, the enjoyment of investing in antiques should have some personality. You're buying a tangible object, you should be able to touch that object, see it in bright sunlight, look at it by candlelight, accept it as part of your life.

I'm reminded of a time long ago, at least twenty-five years ago, when I was working in the only men's clothing store in the little Vermont town where I grew up. The owner of the store was more than my boss, he was a genuinely nice guy and became a friend. Somehow he had wangled himself a part-time job representing a Boston firm of stockbrokers. I don't think he ever sold over fifty shares of stock a week in that town. The town did have two factories, but most of the workers came from outside.

Each morning a few of the factory retirees would drift into the store around ten o'clock and we'd sip coffee and discuss the stock market. The boss, call him Jim, would make a call to Boston to find out how the market was that day. We'd pull out the financial pages of *The New York Times* and read what company was supposed to be about to fold and who was talking merger, and we'd make our choices. I actually bought ten shares of stock one day.

Holding the certificate in my hand was a great feeling. I was actually a stockholder. From then on those morning coffee breaks were business conferences. Jim would call Boston and ask about my stock. I'd wait breathlessly, he'd look at me over his glasses, nod silently, thank the operator, and hang up. I couldn't wait. "Where is it, Jim?" "Up a whole point today, David."

Maybe it was only an $8 stock but to me it was as important as a $300 one. We watched it go up to $12. The retirees all nodded in agreement over their cigars when Jim announced, "Better sell now, it isn't going to go any higher." I did, and watched it slowly slide back to $8. A few months later Jim took me aside and whispered, "It's going to go up again, want to get in?"

I doubled my purchase this time and got in at just over $8 a share. The excitement was back at coffee-break time. Three months later we held a conference. Jim and the retirees said it was time to sell. The stock had passed $12 again. I was holding out to see if it would double. Finally one of the oldsters looked me straight in the eye. "Sonny, don't be greedy. Take your damn profit and don't worry about what might have been."

I wish I could say that he was right. It would have been a fitting end to the story. The truth is that I sold for just over $12 and that damn stock went all the way up to $32 when the company was acquired by one of the top ten corporations in America.

There were a lot of lessons learned through that encounter, not the least of which is to never kick about a profit. It could as easily have been a loss. Set yourself a goal and when you reach it, don't be greedy for more. Another is the pleasure and enjoyment of getting involved in the process, of making decisions for yourself. Lastly, I learned that to make a valid decision one needs information. Back then I couldn't get the information in Vermont that the insiders in New York had. Neither could Jim.

Now I try to find out what is happening to the antiques field in New York, Los Angeles, even London, but often the information is dated. I don't play the stock market anymore, that was my only fling. The antiques market provides enough problems. The rules are the same, though. To successfully invest in antiques you must keep abreast of what is going on. But investing in antiques is more than an investment of money — it's the investment of knowledge, of love, and of time well spent.

Courtesy of *Maine Antique Digest*, Waldoboro, Me.

8

Prices and Values

DISCERNING between the price of an antique and its real worth or value is often the major stumbling block to a beginning collector or investor. Very simply, the price of an antique is what the seller asks for it. The potential buyer usually has no way of knowing how the seller arrived at his price. The value of the antique then has to be determined by the buyer.

I buy and sell antiques; my values are different from yours. I evaluate the salability of an antique. I consider the profit factor before buying. You, the collector/investor, might value the piece for its ability to fit into your home or blend with your decor. You might value it because it will fill the void in your collection. The different criteria used in determining values for antiques bring us to the subject of prices.

Let's look at silver as an example. The price of silver is printed daily in most of the major newspapers in America. Yet only occasionally do pieces of antique silver sell for their weight times the daily melting price. Collectors place an additional value on the age, the maker, the style, the provenance, and other sundry factors. Silver is the best example, but other antiques show similar histories. Almost no antique is worth less than a similar object produced today. If we do nothing else, we add a value for age.

Sometimes people experience a rude awakening upon discovering the value of their antiques. I am afraid I once reinforced a lovely lady's suspicions about her late husband's business acumen by letting slip a few figures. I had learned of this lady's antiques-laden house in western New Hampshire from a relative. "She's got some great stuff," he said, "and she's selling it. She's well over eighty, living on food stamps and Social Security. She cooks and heats with wood. Great character and sharp as a whip."

I headed over. She was all he'd said. Later over a cup of tea she asked, "What do you know about clocks?" I hemmed and hawed and finally admitted that I knew a little. (Most dealers do know a little; if you can recognize age and remember a few prices, that's enough to start with.) She looked me in the eye and sighed. "Five years ago my husband put some things out on the porch and stuck a sign up for a porch sale. Two dealers stopped in and bought five clocks." She paused, then went on. "Three of 'em were mantel clocks in oak cases; they all ran, dinged on the hour, too. Two of 'em hung on the wall, didn't run anymore."

I asked her if they had painted-glass panels in the cases. "Yes, they both had that, I forget the scenes though. They were good looking." I began to describe early-nineteenth-century banjo clocks and she nodded in agreement. I was feeling sick to my stomach but knew I had to ask the question. "How much did you get for the clocks?"

"He sold them to the dealers for ten dollars," she said. "Each?" I asked. "Nope, ten dollars total. How much were they worth?" she asked. I tried to get out of answering. She understood my evasions. "It's OK, I know we gave them away. How much?" This happened in the mid 1970s. Now it would have been a much greater figure but finally I answered. "Well, without seeing them I'd have to take a guess." "How much?" "Somewhere over a thousand probably." That's all I did dare say. If he'd sold a really rare banjo clock, it could have been worth over $5000 by itself.

She sighed and whispered, "Darned fool." After a moment she got out of the chair. "Take a look around, if you see something you want, make an offer." I bought from her. I've been buying a few pieces a year ever since. She's a shrewd businesswoman. I'll make an offer, she'll listen, think, and say, "I guess not this time, maybe next time." I've paid way over any published price for some of her stuff, and I've had some real bargains, too.

Sometimes she names a price, but usually I make an offer. I've bought baskets; a signed Woodstock, Vermont, cheese press with all the cheese-making accessories; a painted table from the Shaker community in North Enfield, New Hampshire, signed by a doctor; and some early pewter. I've also made her an offer on a great armed four-slat ladder-back chair dated 1777 that caused her to sit down in the chair and gasp, "That much for this old chair?" I didn't get the chair. The offer was too much and it went to a relative.

When a price is set on an antique, it is with the anticipation that a buyer somewhere will value the offering to the same dollar amount. The reasons for this price may not be readily apparent to the prospective buyer. The usual reason for a specific price on an average antique is that it represents a pre-determined markup for the dealer. Sometimes the price reflects the seller's preference for a particular field. A dealer who specializes draws the discerning buyers for these objects, and prices his stock accordingly.

Occasionally a dealer tries to establish prices for his field. In the past he has felt that offerings of the type he is selling were underpriced. He offers his stock at a more realistic price, at least to his mind more realistic. If the public agrees with him, he will probably establish the new price levels he sought. If they don't, he will bomb and end up owning some over-priced stock.

Many people find that when they sell their antiques, the value they have placed on them is not shared by others. Unfortunately I have witnessed too many times the exit of a consignor from an auction hall and overheard the disillusioned comments, "Oh boy, they really took me in there. Only one fifty for that bureau! And they only paid thirty-seven fifty for Mom's lamp! Why that lamp had to be worth seventy-five dollars anyway."

Obviously the consignor had placed a much higher value on her objects than anyone would pay. Some of this disillusionment could have been avoided if she had asked the auctioneer before the auction for an estimate of what her items would bring. She would have been made aware that her expectations were too high to start with. If your values for your antiques are above what others will pay, then you are bound to be hurt.

How do you set a realistic value for your antiques? That is a complicated question but I'll try to answer it. Remember that basically a realistic value is a price someone will pay for your antique today. It is not the price someone paid for an antique similar to yours. It is not the price paid two years ago for a similar antique. It is not the price paid for an antique sold one thousand miles away at auction. It is the price you can get for your antique today, in the area in which you live.

Actually there are two values for your antique: one is what you can get for it, the other is what you can replace it for. In this chapter we'll only concern ourselves with the former. The latter, the replacement value, will be covered in the next chapter. Remember the economics of the dealer system. No dealer is going to pay you the full retail price for your antique because he has to make a profit to survive. The replacement cost of your antique is the full retail price.

To figure out the value of your antiques, the price you can get for them today, you must take several things into consideration, not the least of which is who will buy them. If you plan to sell to a dealer, remember that you can expect fifty percent to eighty percent of retail in most cases. Your antiques put on the auction block might realize full retail prices but this is doubtful, since dealers make up the majority of the bidders. In any case, what you finally get will be minus the auctioneer's commission. If you decide to ask the full retail price, you will have to advertise and hope to find a buyer who shares your value figure for the pieces.

See what's happened? There are three prices possible. In one case you set a value and then lowered it by a percentage so the piece would sell. In another you let the buyer determine the price. In the last you set a price and stuck to it. But how do you set that first price?

Since antiques first started being collected and sold, records of their prices have been kept. One can check these records and find the asking or selling price for almost anything. Sometimes you'll have to dig long and hard to find what you're looking for, but it's there. Eventually these records began to be compiled in books which we've come to know as price guides.

From the very start you should not consider a price guide as a Bible; what you find there is not written in stone. The most common complaint heard from dealers about retail customers concerns the misuse of price guides. Start with the very words "price guides." I don't care what they are called — price lists, auction records, buying guides, official buying records, or anything else — they are *guides,* they help to point the way, and that's all they do. This book is also a guide, I am pointing the way, but I can't do it all for you. You have to take the information offered, digest it, and apply it yourself.

What can a price guide do for you? It can tell you what a piece was sold for, or what price was being asked for a piece, sometime, somewhere, and in some condition. You have one tiny bit of information about the piece. You may not know when the price was established, who established it, what condition the piece was in, or where or under what conditions the price was set. You may not know who collected the information or why.

Don't kid yourself, every one of those factors is important. Was the price established a year ago or three months ago? Was it an asking price, a selling price, or an auction price? Was the price asked by a big dealer at an important show, or by a country dealer at an out-of-the-way shop? Is it a New York City price or an Ohio price? Was the piece in perfect condition? Did it have replaced parts? Was the piece from a famous collection? Did it sell at a highly publicized auction or just a run-of-the-mill one? Did the writer actually compile the prices himself or did dealers send him a list of prices? Did the compiler have a reason for compiling the prices, such as trying to establish new prices for items he himself is selling?

A good price guide will answer some if not all of these questions in its introduction. A look through the guide will reveal where, when, and how. If questions still remain, you have to decide whether this guide is for you. Is it relevant to your piece at all? Treat a price guide as a guide. It does give you somewhere to start. Once you have that price in front of you, start asking yourself the list of questions.

Compare the prices in the dealers' shops in your area with the ones in the guide, but here's a tip. Don't walk into a shop with a price guide in your hand. It identifies you as a neophyte immediately. Find a piece similar to yours and remember the price. Do this in several shops. Compare these prices to those listed in the price guide. Now you have an idea of how valid this specific price guide is for your area.

Dealers are going to hate me for suggesting you do this. That's natural — they are in business to sell antiques, not provide a free pricing service, but you do it already. Most dealers would rather you set a realistic value for your pieces than have an inflated idea of their worth. Please, for your own sake, be discreet, don't bring in a list and go through their stock marking down prices. Make certain you visit several dealers so that you get an adequate sampling of area prices. Check out the auctions too; you may find prices vary significantly from those in the shops.

It's a common sight here in New England to sit behind a price-guide-clutching beginner at auction. You watch the frantic thumbing through pages, hear the whispered dialogue.

"The next item he's going to sell is that cup and saucer you liked."

"Who's the maker?"

"I don't know. Wait — there, he said 'Clews.' Quick, look it up!"

"Clews, Clews, here it is. There are three of them listed. What pattern?"

"He didn't say. Quick, the bidding is up to one hundred. Should I bid?"

"Go ahead, the cheapest one in here is one sixty. Put up your hand, quick! Ah, that's it. He saw you. Who else is bidding?"

"That woman over there, oh damn, she's gone up to one fifty. He wants one seventy-five now. George! What'll I do?"

"Bid, bid quick! There's one here in the price guide for two fifty!"

"That woman's got it up to two hundred, should I keep

bidding?''

"Go on, keep going, go right up to two fifty if you have to. It must be worth that if she's still bidding, and there is one in here for two fifty.''

Sometimes I can envision a little scenario that might happen later. I can imagine this couple walking into an area antiques shop and viewing an identical cup and saucer priced — quite fairly, too, by area standards — at $140. I can see their crestfallen faces as they listen in amazement when the dealer explains that she doesn't know where the price guide got those prices. "Around here,'' she explains, "one forty, one fifty is the top dealers can get for that piece. Lord knows, I'd like to get more, but I've had this one for a year now and no takers.''

Before you begin the pricing procedure, you must carefully match up your piece with an example in the price guide. For many, this is the hardest part. Let's take an example. We'll suppose you have a pressed-pattern glass water pitcher that was your grandmother's. To start with, we'll assume you can tell it's pressed glass, not cut or blown. You've read a few of the books on glass and know that pressed glass is the most common type. You recognize the heavy weight and sharp edges of cut glass. You know what the bottom of a blown-glass piece should look like. Yours is like neither of these types. You look for and recognize the ridges or lines that indicate a piece was pressed in a mold.

Through the use of any one of the books on pattern glass available at your local bookstore or library you identify the pattern. You have a water pitcher in the Royal Ivy pattern made by the Northwood Glass Company in Ohio in 1889 or 1890. You check a couple of price guides. One lists three different colors and prices. The other has one price listed and doesn't mention the color. If you can match a color listed, use that price as a base. If not, take the lowest price as a base. Any dealer to whom you offer your pitcher will do the same.

Now I'm going to give you a real problem. You have a quilt on the guest bed upstairs. A weekend guest arrives with his pet poodle. Saturday morning he looks you sheepishly in the eye and announces that the dog tore the quilt to shreds. He offers to reimburse you for the quilt and can well afford to. You pull out the price guide.

You know your quilt was the wedding-ring pattern but when you look up the pattern in the price guide the prices run all over the place. What to do? In this case the price guide becomes as valuable as a square wheel on a wheelbarrow. Condition, age, design, color, and attractiveness determine a quilt's value. The mere recording of a price for a pattern or color is worthless. You had best plan a shopping trip to antiques shops for Saturday afternoon. What the price guide did do was indicate that early quilts, and signed and dated examples, were worth more than others.

How about furniture? Provided you can accurately date and type your antique furniture, will a price guide help you set the value? The answer is a very qualified yes, or if you prefer, a slightly qualified no. Furniture will bring a price because of such a variety of factors that using only a listing in a price guide without referring to all the other factors is of minimal value. A pictured price guide is a little more help than a simple listing in an unpictured one because you can at least compare your piece with the picture.

Condition, repairs, form, finish — all are of paramount importance when dealing with furniture. You have to treat listings for antique furniture in a price guide as a newspaper reporter would: consider who, what, where, and when. Is there any value to the listings then? Yes, there is. You can use them as a guide. They will tell you that a dry sink with a cupboard back is worth more than one without it. They will tell you that a Chippendale chair is worth more than an oak pressed-back chair.

They give you a guide to the varying types of furniture. They show you that pieces with original decoration or intact finishes bring more than refinished pieces. If you have no knowledge of furniture types and styles, a price guide is useless. Without full disclosure to you of what the piece being priced is and where and when the price was set, the same disclaimer applies.

I have never used a price guide to buy or sell a piece of furniture. Never. Every piece is different. A dealer may start with a basic figure in mind for a specific piece and then upgrade or downgrade the price until he arrives at a figure. His final figure takes into consideration the area he sells in, his experience with the type or form he's looking at, the salability of the piece, and his own like or dislike of it.

So how do you set a value on your furniture if the price guide is of so little use? First, you must know just what you have. Read Chapters 1 and 2 on furniture types and periods. Above all, read the books listed there. Become familiar with furniture. When you are ready to positively identify your pieces, check the price guides. Can you find your pieces there? Now check the shops. What are similar pieces selling for? Attend the auctions. All this time keep comparing your pieces with those pieces you see. Price your pieces up or down accordingly. It isn't easy. You have to either do it this way or have a professional do it for you.

Do I think price guides are worthwhile? Yes, I do. They become especially valuable when used to price the easily identifiable factory-produced antiques. I know many dealers who would be lost without their price guides.

If you want immediate information on a whole spectrum of antiques prices, the price guide is a must. There are numerous guides on the market. Some are highly specialized, especially those that deal with twentieth century collectibles. A general rule of thumb is that the newer the object being collected, the more accurate the price guide.

Perusing the antiques reference section of the local book stores recently, I found an array of price guides. There's probably a price guide for your specialty, whether it be dolls, art-deco jewelry, baseball cards, Oriental ceramics, historical Staffordshire, cut glass, paintings, or musical instruments. Rather than carry many specialized guides, most dealers prefer to use one general price guide. There are three that I see used most often in New England.

The Kovels' Antiques Price List by Ralph and Terry Kovel (Crown Publishing) is probably the most popular. There are

45,000 computer-set listings in the current copy. It's a bit difficult for a novice to get used to, but with practice one learns how to use the listings. For example, silver souvenir spoons don't come under the heading of Silver, plate, or Silver, American, and there is no spoon listing. Look under Souvenir. This is a good general price guide. It is fairly up to date, for some listings are only a few months old when it is published each year.

All price guides share a common failing. No matter how accurate a price guide is at publication (and here *Kovels'* has an edge because its computer format allows it to include relatively recent prices), by the time a guide is around for the full year, some prices are hopelessly outdated. For many items this doesn't matter, they show small fluctuations in value from year to year anyway; for others the lag could be deadly.

Take the example of weather vanes. A few years ago they caught on with collectors and in one year prices skyrocketed. The city prices trickled out to the country. Anyone armed with a price guide could have paid full retail prices and more to owners of weather vanes and have immediately doubled his money.

Anyone using a price guide, be it dealer or collector, should make certain he is using the latest edition. If you are sitting at an auction using a three-year-old price guide, you will buy damn little. Your old price guides do have some value though. If you can find the same item in them for several years, you can chart the rise or fall of your antique's price.

Another price guide that has gained wide acceptance is *Warman's Fifteenth Antiques and Their Prices,* edited by P.S. Warman (Warman Publishing). There will probably be a sixteenth edition by the time you read this, even though the company has been sold and Harry Rinker is now editor. *Warman's* gives good descriptions of the categories listed — slightly better than *Kovels',* in fact. It is popular with glass collectors because of its listing of reproduced items. The prices given are averages of prices recorded and are generally accurate for an average example.

To show how deceptive any price guide can be, a 1975

edition of *Warman's* guide lists weather vanes at $400 to $650. Those were pretty accurate prices then. A 1980-81 edition of *Kovels'* lists them at $27.50 to $1350. Neither describes any of the listings as reproductions. I would love to buy at the *Kovels'* prices, but without seeing the weather vanes (and that means more than just looking at a photograph), it's impossible to know what the listed prices mean.

A general price guide that is beginning to win acceptance with collectors is the *Pictorial Price Guide to American Antiques* by Dorothy Hammond (E.P. Dutton). My copy is the second, 1979, edition, but there is now a new edition in print. Hammond does something that neither of the others does. She illustrates every object listed. This makes for a large-format book that won't fit into a big coat pocket like the others, but some people prefer the pictures. She obtains her listings from auctions and dealers, and tells you where and when. Replacements, damage, and refinishing are noted. There aren't as many listings as in the others, but the descriptions are better.

There you have it. Yes, there are other general price guides but these three are my favorites. For one thing, they try to cover a wide geographic area. Sometimes I find a subject heavy on midwestern prices, other times I note a New England bias, but in general I can average them. If you buy a price guide that deals only with a specific area, you may be sorry, unless experience proves it's valid for your area.

The one factor that no price guide can begin to cover is attachment. For example, it's not uncommon for a dealer to visit someone's house to look over the grouping of antiques being offered. He carefully considers the top prices for which the items can be sold, perhaps even consulting a price guide. Finally he makes an offer, only to be greeted by the seller's looks of amazement and firm rejection. What happened?

If your emotional tie to your antiques is strong, there is no way a dealer can estimate a price for them. Let me qualify that. If you have no understanding of antiques values and your idea of prices greatly outstrips the offer made, the transaction is over — a buyer can't pay extra for attachment.

When we flip open a price guide and I say, "Look, here

on page 402, a milk-glass three-kittens plate, twenty dollars. That's the selling price. I offered fifteen. I have to make some profit,'' only to hear you reply, ''Nope, that was Aunt Sarah's. I'd have to get at least fifty dollars to part with it!'' there is nothing more to say. You have $30 worth of attachment to that plate. Maybe someday, if you live long enough, the price will catch up to your value. If you really want to sell the plate, I hope it does.

I don't mean to disparage your attachment to your antiques, not in the least. We all have items we wouldn't part with for love or money. But when you come to sell your antiques, remember that you are dealing with a business that places prices on antiques for a variety of reasons, attachment not being one of them.

While you are leafing through the price guides, you will probably notice a wide disparity of price between two similar items. The guide doesn't note any difference in descriptions. Both may be listed as ''set of six nineteenth-century Pennsylvania painted country-pine chairs.'' One set is listed at $600, the other $2400. Why? Remember what I wrote about demand determining price? If both prices were auction prices, obviously there was $1800 worth of more demand for one set than for the other.

The demand is set by the quality of the antique being offered. In the case of the two identically listed sets of chairs, the higher-priced set might have had great form, wonderfully folksy original bright paint, and no repairs or replacements. The other might have been simply a plain set of country chairs with either very worn or new paint.

A price guide can rarely indicate the quality of the item being listed. Sometimes this can be inferred by the price listed, but a high price does not always indicate quality.

Picking the one great piece out of the welter of the average is a knack that the more successful dealers and collectors acquire. It takes a lot of experience and understanding of antiques to get to the point where you just know that this one piece is worth five or six times the average piece. Price is always tied directly to demand, and demand is tied to quality.

The quality pieces bring those record prices you read about. It's difficult to teach anyone to recognize quality. You must be willing to study the average antique first to recognize the great one. And I think you have to love antiques to undertake this kind of study.

At a Vermont flea market one summer Sunday, I bought the best coconut-shell dipper I've ever owned. These dippers were made by sailors from coconuts they picked up while on cruises in the Pacific. The one I bought was made in the middle of the nineteenth century. (They're difficult to positively date any closer than that.) What made mine above average, besides the original turned wooden handle and the heart-shaped pewter mount, was the fully carved face decorating the coconut shell.

What was more astonishing than the carving was the price — $2. This piece of folk art had been sitting on the seller's table for over five hours when I bought it. A lot of dealers had passed it by. One had even greeted my late arrival at the flea market with, "Nothing here today, all sold out."

Don't start feeling sorry for the seller; when you put a price on your offering, it is up for grabs. If I had walked into your house and been asked to make an offer on that piece, I'd have gone over $200. If you price your antiques, you are offering to sell them at that price. Any dealer could have picked up that dipper, and should have. It isn't easy to price quality or rarity but if you have antiques to sell, or that you value, you should learn how.

The price guides will provide the base. Then you must visit the shops and auctions; compare, upgrade, downgrade. Look at the pieces bringing the high prices. Ask questions, read the magazines, visit the museums, look at the great collections. You will start to know when paint becomes more than simple decoration, when a form soars above the ordinary. Don't expect to acquire this ability from just a couple of books. It takes time, but it's worth it.

Photo by Edward J. Lucas, Jr.

9

Protecting Yourself

PROTECTING yourself after purchasing antiques is different from protecting yourself when buying, for example, a new car. You knew what to do when you bought the new Mercedes. The dealer explained the warranty. You understood the need for periodic checkups and maintenance visits. You bought the appropriate insurance. You knew that the car was listed in a value book used by all the insurance agencies. Well, friend, antiques are different.

Whether it's an antique you are buying for use in your home, or the beginning of a collection, you should protect yourself from the very start — when you actually make the purchase. Always get a signed and dated sales slip from the dealer from whom you buy. Make sure the sales slip accurately describes the item bought — along with any repairs, restorations, etc. — and states whether or not the item is original. If, after future scrutiny, the item turns out not to be what is stated, this sales slip is your only protection.

An honest dealer will take back a piece that is incorrectly described. Small repairs not noted can cause problems but major restorations, large repairs, etc., not noted will usually prompt the seller to refund the purchase price. This applies to most dealers. If you bought at a flea market or from a dealer in a distant state at an antiques show, problems could arise. Auctions vary in their guarantees. Read the auction catalogue carefully. Usually it is a case of "let the buyer beware." If you bid on something and win it, you own it.

Remember that no one likes to refund money. A small dealer has usually already invested the money in another purchase. If the piece isn't what you thought you were buying, the burden of proof will fall on you. The sales slip then becomes of paramount value. If it states you were buying a Queen Anne-style desk for $2000 and you find it's a 1900 copy, you are out of luck. Remember, "Queen Anne-style" doesn't mean that the piece was made in the Queen Anne period (1720-1755), it only means that the piece is of the style produced during that period. From the evidence of that sales slip I doubt you would ever convince any judge or jury that you didn't get what you bought.

I hope that you will never have to get to that stage in a return process. You must know what you are buying. Protecting yourself should actually start with acquiring some knowledge of antiques before going out there and throwing your money around. Most dealers are honest and will describe their merchandise correctly. It is too much to hope that they are all honest, though, and if you persist in buying without any knowledge of antiques, you will get stung sooner or later. Still, a correct sales slip may save you.

Keep those sales slips with your other valuable records in a secure place, preferably in a safe or safe-deposit box. They aren't of much value in proving loss if they burn up along with the antiques. Concerning fire, you probably have a homeowner's or renter's insurance policy covering the contents of your house. Contact your insurance agency before you get heavily into collecting. If you wish to cover your antiques, you will probably have to add an antiques floater or fine-arts rider to your existing policy.

If you are starting an investment collection or have inherited antiques, contact that insurance agency immediately. Get a policy in effect as soon as possible. Art and antiques thefts are on the rise.

At this point you may find that some of the things you can do to satisfy the insurance company will still not totally protect you. You call in an appraiser who lists your antiques and their values (more about appraisers later, it's a complicated subject). A copy of the appraisal will go to the insurance company. You check the locks on the doors and windows and change any that need replacing. You install smoke alarms, check your wiring, and have the furnace inspected. Feel safe now?

Sorry. If a thief really wants to steal your antiques, there is very little you can do to stop him. Burglar alarms can slow him down, leaving lights on may hinder him, a barking dog may make him figure out another method, but a truly professional criminal can still get to those antiques. Thank God that there aren't that many professionals. Taking the above steps will stop the teenager or non-professional, and I highly recommend you do so if you feel the value of your antiques warrants such action.

Friends of mine in New York City found that the combination of an alarm system and a guard dog finally halted the loss of their antiques. They can live with the inconvenience of the system and the cost of the dog but maybe you can't. What then? Do you have to accept the inevitability of the theft of your antiques?

Not totally. You can accept the possibility that they might be stolen and take steps before the theft to insure that they will be recovered. Before the theft, you ask? Yes, that's the only time you can do it; after they're gone is too late. What you have to do is make sure that your antiques can be absolutely, positively identified as your property.

You must photograph and describe your antiques in detail, and store all of this information with those other valuable papers. By a photograph I don't mean a fuzzy Polaroid. Unless you are a near-professional photographer I recommend that you spend a bit extra and have a professional do the job. You want a clear, easily reproducible photo that shows in sharp detail all the features of your antique. You may need several photos for a single piece of furniture.

With the photos you need a detailed description of the salient features. Describe missing veneer, damage to a leg, replaced parts, condition of the finish, any unusual marks or stains — anything that differentiates your piece from similar pieces. Don't just *describe* a piece of furniture. List the little things that make your piece different. It's important. The average police hot sheet reads like a price guide. There may be a mahogany Sheraton table with reeded legs listed but what I as a dealer want to know if I'm offered a similar piece is that there is an hourglass-shaped ink stain on the corner of a leaf on the stolen one.

Maybe what you are thinking at this point is that if unusual details will identify your pieces, why not go the whole route and mark your pieces with your name or Social Security number? You could do that. You could do that if you don't plan on ever selling them, or leaving them in your will to someone who will sell them. You see, when a dealer is offered a piece with the owner's name or number etched or scratched firmly into it, he begins to wonder. Is this piece stolen? Sure he can try to research the number, but the Social Security Administration won't release those names to just anybody. Usually the dealer has to take a chance. Often he won't. If he does, it is at a far lower price than that he'd offer for an unmarked piece.

There's the problem of the future owner too. Does he scratch or gouge out the number or name of the former owner and find a place to put his own on the piece? That scratch or gouge has lowered the value again. There's also the question about a piece with a gouged-out area. Is it a stolen piece? If you are determined to sign your antiques, do it with the knowledge that you are removing them from the marketplace or lowering their value drastically.

To illustrate the problem of Social Security-marked pieces, consider this. A few years ago I looked at two fine pewter whale-oil lamps in a small shop in rural Virginia. Both had a lovely old patina and were good examples of mid-nineteenth-century lighting. The price was a very low $100 each. I wondered why. When I turned them over the answer became obvious. Deeply engraved on the bottom of both was the Social Security number of the former owner. The shopkeeper said sadly, "I don't know why no one has bought these, they are way under priced. My dealer price is only eighty each. They're not stolen. I bought them from the woman who put the number on them."

I was sorely tempted to buy them, but any dealer would have had the same reservations I had. This seller might have known that she bought them from the legitimate owner but how about the next? People are extremely wary of the possibility of stolen antiques, and rightfully so. I didn't have a private collector of pewter waiting for the lamps right then, so I passed them up. If they hadn't been marked, I could have sold them for a quick $250 each.

There *is* a way to mark your possessions without hurting their value. You have to choose a surface that won't show and place an unobtrusive mark there. On the bottom of a pair of brass candlesticks you file a small "x" or two lines, or something similar. You note this mark on your description sheet. You mark the back edge of a drawer side. You put three ink dots on the back edge of the frame surrounding your antique sampler.

You want the police or dealer to be able to identify your antiques without hurting their value or allowing the thief the chance to remove the mark. Remember that a thief doesn't mind filling in your numbers with solder or gouging a number out. He may sell the items at a fraction of their value anyway. Too obvious a mark invites removal.

If the antiques are stolen, you must get these descriptions of identifying marks to the prospective purchasers as soon as possible. Ask the police if they are circulating descriptions to the local dealers and auctioneers. If they aren't, do it yourself. Once a dealer has been alerted to the theft of your antiques, he can't ignore them when and if they are offered to him. Because stolen antiques are quite often trucked far away from the area in which they were stolen, it's necessary to alert the shops across the country, too. To do this you may have to notify the national magazines serving the antiques industry.

Some of them will list your stolen antiques cost free. But if the list is long and you want to include photos, you may have to purchase space. Get the most space you can afford and list those marks and descriptions. Some of the monthly news magazines have an amazingly long shelf life. The dealers and collectors pull out those back issues and read and reread them.

163

If your photos are clear and the markings are unique, there is a good chance someone will eventually spot one of your pieces.

The police will then start backtracking from buyer to seller until somebody fails to come up with a sales slip. You may not recover all your antiques but you can rejoice in the knowledge that one thief caught is one more out of business.

It's a lot of work to recover your stolen antiques. It costs money, too. If you carry the antiques floater on your homeowner's insurance policy and know that the insurance company will pay one-hundred percent of their appraised value, why try to recover? For many people, antiques aren't just household furnishings, they are family heirlooms, loved and cherished possessions. They represent more than money.

Just as I can't put a value on your attachment to your antiques when I come to your house and offer to buy them, so may you find that the money an insurance company pays you when they're stolen isn't enough. People used to wander through my shop looking for a table "like the one we had stolen."

I might have had a pine drop-leaf table that fitted the description but somehow it never quite fitted the need. If you truly love your antiques, money won't replace them. You must protect them before they're stolen. Maybe you should mark them. Even if you don't, you should photograph and accurately describe them.

I am sorry to have to tell you that if your antique is not unique or well marked, the odds of getting it back are very low. One ironstone platter is a lot like another. A dealer who buys one like yours from a picker doesn't have much to worry about when you come in and exclaim, "Oh, that looks just like my platter that was stolen last month!" That it looks like yours doesn't prove a thing. There are thousands out there that look like yours. If the dealer says he bought it at a flea market for cash and didn't get a sales slip, so what?

You stand a fighting chance of recovering well-marked, highly identifiable antiques that are stolen, but the odds diminish considerably on mass-produced items. The police may stop a truck full of antiques and find that every item corresponds exactly with your list of stolen antiques, but don't count on it. And once these items are separated from each other and pass through several hands, the odds of recovering them become even lower. Maybe you should think about buying that guard dog.

When you visited the insurance agency and explained that you had a lot of antiques you wanted to insure, they undoubtedly told you that you would have to have them appraised. Even if you have an appraisal sheet from some years back, you should have an up-to-date appraisal done. Antiques values change constantly. You could suffer a substantial loss collecting according to an out-of-date appraisal.

Where do you go to get an appraisal? If you call the guy down the street with the truck painted "Antiques Bought and Sold, Auctioneer and Appraiser," you could be in big trouble. This guy may be one of the people you will want to call if you decide to sell your antiques, but for an insurance appraisal you need someone whose figures will be accepted by your insurance company. You want those figures to be accurate, up to date, and truly representative of the replacement cost of your antiques.

An appraisal of your antiques is nothing more than an educated guess but you want it to be as educated as possible. An appraiser's estimate of your antiques' worth depends on his experience as well as his knowledge of antiques, the current state of the market, and prevailing prices. Perhaps the guy down the street is well versed in these areas, maybe he isn't. Ask your insurance agency if they have an appraiser they prefer to use. Better still, write the American Society of Appraisers, Dulles International Airport, P.O. Box 17625, Washington, DC 20041, and ask for the names of appraisers in your area.

There is a good reason for this search for a competent appraiser. There are a lot of people who have found that by advertising appraisals they have gained access to a house full of antiques. Oh, they will do the appraisal, but they will usually also walk out with at least one antique at their price. They'll tell you what everything is worth and keep pushing the fact that they will pay so much for a piece. When an appraiser offers to buy your antique for the figure he's appraised it at, beware; he hasn't given you an accurate appraisal or a full retail price. Also avoid an appraiser who offers to swap his services for goods. Some of these so-called appraisers are extremely adept at changing your no to a yes. Make it very clear that you have called the appraiser for appraising only and you don't want to sell anything.

You should make it clear from the minute you hire an appraiser what you want the appraisal for. An appraisal for insurance purposes is based on the replacement value of your antiques. The value of your antiques based on what they would bring if sold is a different story. It's far less than the replacement value. Usually this type of appraisal is done to value an estate. Just remember that even with an appraisal for the cash value of your antiques, a good appraiser will not offer to buy them for his appraised price. It's against the code of ethics.

How does the appraiser-buyer work? Remember the story about the door-knocker in the first chapter? The appraiser-buyer is today's counterpart of that guy. The only thing that's different is where the door-knocker worked on cold leads (he went from door to door, uninvited), you've actually invited the appraiser-buyer in, and he is glad of it.

Pad and pencil in hand, he follows you from room to room, noting the items you point out, and entering a price for each on his pad. Where the honest appraiser would have to spend some time figuring values (perhaps consulting his library and taking a few days to come up with a price), this guy wants to get it over with right there.

He shows you his figures, then mentions that he'd be willing to take antiques in trade for his fee. If you state, "No, I'm only interested in getting my antiques appraised," he'll ask if you care to sell any of them. Now he starts his hard-sell routine.

"Look, these figures are very fair. I doubt that you'd find any dealer around here who would give you close to what I appraised them at. Tell you what I'm going to do, though. I like you, you've got a nice house here. There's a couple of pieces on this list that my wife collects. How about doing me a favor and selling them to me? I'd really like to surprise her with them. I mean, really, I took time out of a real busy day to come over here and give you a good high appraisal. Now you can do me one little favor, can't you? I'll give you the full appraisal price. No other dealer would do that."

It's a hard spiel to ignore. In a large percentage of their calls, appraiser-buyers leave with at least one antique. You have to stick to your guns.

For many years the most common type of appraiser has been the so-called general one. This individual was able to go through the whole house, giving appraisals for everything from the china in the corner cupboard to the quilts on the beds. He had his parallel in the now-departed general practitioner of the medical field. And just like the general practitioner, he has been superseded by the specialist.

The antiques industry, like the world it exists in, is fragmenting into a world of special interests. It makes sense to seek an appraiser who specializes in Oriental china if that is what you have inherited from your Great-Aunt Harriet. There are general appraisers still offering their services. You may want to contact them if your antiques run the gamut from soup bowls to nutcrackers. It certainly would be cheaper than bringing in an array of specialists.

The cost of an appraisal is not the primary concern; the accuracy of the appraisal should be paramount. The costs are usually fairly even within a given area. Most charge by the hour with a flat fee as a minimum. If an appraiser lives out of your area, you will usually have to pay a travel fee.

What you should really worry about is the ability of the appraiser to price your antiques at today's standards. If he's using a price guide, it must accurately represent the area in which you live, not a state hundreds of miles away. He must know what pieces are selling for at local auctions and what they bring at city auctions, and must explain which standard he is using for his appraisals.

What you want from the appraiser and how he is going to do it have to be discussed. Think of the process as somewhat akin to choosing a garage to have major work done on your car. Shop around.

Taking care of those antiques you've inherited or collected very rightfully has to come under the heading of protecting yourself. You've made some wise choices in buying them. You're going to drive a hard bargain when selling. What are you going to do with them while you own them?

In most cases you should do the very minimum required to keep them in the condition they were in when you bought them. This means you dust them, you wash them if they're dirty, you keep them warm in the winter and cool in the summer, and other than that you let them alone.

More antiques are ruined by well-meaning attempts to clean them, or improve them, than by anything else I can think of. Remember that these articles are antiques, they are at least one hundred years old, and they should show their age. If you must have bright, spotless, pristine virgins about your house, buy reproductions. Antiques have nicks, dents, scratches, worn areas, and a build-up of surfaces (called patina) caused by age. These signs of age often determine an antique's value. Don't remove them.

There are some things you can do to protect the condition of your antiques. Furniture suffers greatly from changes in weather. Wood swells with a rise in humidity and shrinks in dry weather. Antique furniture often is found with cracks in veneer and looseness in joints from these climatic changes. Using a humidifier helps immensely during New England heating seasons. You may live in an area that is going to require a dehumidifier during summer months. Try to maintain a stable atmosphere year-round to insure the least damage to antique furniture.

Do as little as you can to the finish of antique furniture. Wipe up food or drink spills as soon as they happen. Use only water or, at the very most, a mild dish detergent. Use coasters under alcoholic drinks. If you or your guests insist on drinking around antique furniture, sooner or later the furniture finish is going to suffer. Alcohol lifts old varnish, causes stains, and raises hell with the finish. Maybe you should apply a coat of Minwax Hard Oil Finish as soon as you buy a piece. It is alcohol resistant and seals the old finish. If you are going to use the piece where alcoholic beverages are consumed, it may be a necessity.

Don't use a strong detergent on painted country furniture either. I damn near ruined a red painted blanket chest one night by trying to wash it. Old buttermilk paint will lift off very easily.

Polish only with a good grade paste wax. Avoid the spray waxes you can buy in a supermarket as they will remove the patina. If you insist on polishing the old hardware on a piece of furniture, take it off to do so since most brass polishes will damage the wood surface.

There's one thing to remember about any metal polish. If it leaves a dark color on the polishing cloth during the rubbing, it is removing some of the metal. This doesn't hurt much when doing brass or copper, but eventually could be serious with silver or pewter. Buy the softest, or most non-scouring polish available. Most collectors prefer copper and brass to be bright. It is permissible to polish it.

There are differing opinions about polishing silver. Purists prefer it with its patina and hold that any polishing removes that patina. They prefer to keep it in tarnish-proof bags. The average collector likes to see it brightly shining on display. If you *must* polish, use the gentlest of polishes and cloths.

Pewter in its period was as brightly polished as silver is today. Now we find it with its dark grey patina. Don't do anything to it. Force yourself to leave it alone.

Antique fabrics are extremely tricky objects. Rugs can be carefully vacuumed but washing any old fabric is very hazardous. Never put an antique quilt into an automatic washer or dryer. Some of the old dyes were made of vegetable matter and are not colorfast. I once saw a quilt that started life as red and white but had turned a uniform pink. If you have to clean antique fabric, seek a specialist. Look for a listing in an antiques publication for a fabric conservationist.

Most people are aware that paintings can be cleaned. Every now and then I run across one that was cleaned with a home formula. I've seen potatoes used, garage-grade hand soap, and beer, and even heard of a guy who used Lysol. They all make interesting stories but, sad to say, they will ruin an oil painting. I've cleaned paintings, there is an easy enough method, but even that is not totally safe. Old varnish can be removed, but it is not a job for an amateur.

Stick to vacuuming the surface with a soft brush attachment. If the varnish has darkened with age, take the painting to a restorer. It is not a terribly expensive job to remove the varnish and it makes a world of difference to the painting. I'm not going to tell you how to do it. If even one reader ruins a valuable painting, it is not worth it.

I recently previewed an auction and there among the offerings was what once was a very nice signed Dutch floral still life, oil on canvas. Someone had stripped the old varnish and revarnished the canvas. The paint was removed through to the base color in many places and in some areas the canvas was showing. Painting restoration is no job for an amateur.

With all your antiques you should only do that which is absolutely necessary to maintain them. If you choose pieces that are in top shape to start with, try to keep them in that shape. Resist those urges to improve on that condition.

If your antiques do suffer damage and you wish to attempt their repair yourself, there is one book that can help. *The Antique Restorer's Handbook* by George Grotz (Doubleday) is well written and offers many useful formulas for the do-it-yourselfer. One word of advice: before you start any repair project, try out the process on a practice piece.

Protecting yourself while buying, keeping, and selling antiques involves the same degree of common sense you should use in any other aspect of life. If, when you put together your antiques collection, you are willing to exercise the same caution you expend on other purchases, you're on the right track to protecting yourself.

Photos by Ginny Caputo

10

Collectibles and Flea Markets

THERE is one kind of collecting that hasn't been touched upon so far. This is the field of collectibles. Collectibles are that broad class of objects that, while not strictly classified as antiques, are avidly collected by a wide-spread group of collectors. Collectibles can include everything from buttons to depression glass, and are usually of twentieth-century origin.

There are collectors of calendars, comic books, coloring books, cap pistols, car parts, coin-price guides, and candy containers. Every time I think I've heard about the most absurd item being collected, along comes another collector and his field to top it. Collectibles are fun. The buyers usually operate in the low-priced field since being able to afford an item certainly does liven up the search.

It's not an unprofitable field, either. Many collectors have put together an amazing collection in a very few years only to see other collectors join in the search, and the resulting demand boosts the value of their collection to new levels. Many dealers started out as collectors.

I had dabbled with antiques for a few years, with a little buying and selling around the fringes of the business, but it took a bottle collection to catapult me right into the heart of dealing. During deer-hunting season in Vermont some years ago, a friend informed me he'd stumbled onto an abandoned farm dump back in the hills. He'd been pulling bottles out of the ground, boxing them up, and selling them to an antiques dealer for what seemed like high figures. Now his car was out of commission and did I want to go digging bottles for half the take?

A mild December morning found us high up in the Vermont hill country among the ruins of the farm, which appeared to have been abandoned in the 1920s. The dump lay at one end of a field with a very cold brook running alongside the outer edge. The brook had eroded part of the dump and the refuse rested there in layers just waiting to be picked over.

That first day we hauled out nearly twenty boxes of bottles of all kinds and colors. I knew nothing, absolutely nothing, about bottles. I guessed that the majority of the ones we were digging out dated from before 1900, but it was only a guess. When we arrived at the dealer's shop, he and his wife rushed out to help us unload. Bottles rattled and tinkled from the trunk and floor of my car.

The dealer's wife muttered something about taking better care of the bottles and he glared at her. They asked what we wanted for them. My friend Jim quickly answered, "Same as before, four dollars a box. Eighty bucks total." I knew something was up from the quickness with which the four twenties were passed to us.

That night I went to the library. Later, much later, I was banging on Jim's door to tell him what kind of bottles we were selling and what the retail prices could be. "So what," he said. "If they can get that kind of money, more power to them. All I know is that's pretty good pay for a few hours' work. If you want to keep your half of what we find, go ahead."

Next morning I was looking at the material in the dump in a new light. We had been lucky, we were in the "earliest" part of the dump. I carefully sorted through the pickings to fill my share of the boxes.

I've never seen a dump since that was in such an untouched condition. Blown flasks, demijohns, colored-glass perfumes, early canning jars — all there just waiting to be picked out of the ground. I even found an 1853 half dollar that had been made into a love token by filing off the surface on one side and engraving in flowery Victorian script, "To My Darling Sarah."

A few days later it all came to an end. Someone had come in over the weekend and systematically uprooted the whole place. What they didn't take they broke.

Just writing about that dump brings back the thrill of the material that was there. I'm a lot older and more experienced now but I'd give a lot to go back to that first morning again. We sold an awful lot of great bottles for $4 a box.

The rest of that winter I washed and catalogued my finds. By March I'd weeded out the common examples and was left with the nucleus of a bottle collection. In April another friend told me of the impending demolition of the old family home. The house was over a mile back in the woods on a one-lane dirt road long since abandoned by the town. The land had been sold to some summer people, the house was rotting away on its foundation, and it was scheduled to be bulldozed and burned any day. If I wanted anything out of the house, I'd have to move fast.

He hadn't lied about the condition of the place. Window-less and doorless, it stood in the middle of a high field with a great view to the south and of Massachusetts. We entered gingerly. The center of every room gaped rottenly down to the cellar. We got up to the attic by tiptoeing on the outer edges of the deteriorated stairs. While there had been nothing of value left downstairs the attic was another story. Ladder-back chairs lined one wall. A pine pewter hutch stood on its bootjack cut-out base in a corner. Three walnut parlor organs were against another wall.

We easily removed the chairs and the hutch to his truck but the organs were difficult. Finally I suggested we take them out through the attic window. We kicked out the remainder of the window casing, attached a rope to the chimney, and pro-ceeded to move the first organ to the window. Strange noises began to come from the chimney as the rope tightened. Sud-denly, with a great roar the whole chimney plunged straight down two floors to the cellar, and stranger still, the rope held, and the organ followed the chimney through a gigantic hole in the attic floor to vanish in a cloud of dust. Two very shaken people got the hell out of that house as soon as possible. By the time I'd figured out a way to get the remaining two organs, the house had been bulldozed and burned, organs and all.

Late spring found me setting up on the flea-market circuit with a bottle collection and my pine furniture. As the pieces sold I had to replace my stock. I was never lucky enough to get my stock free of charge again.

Flea markets are still a good place for the collector to search. Some provide a variety of genuine antiques but the average flea market nowadays is more apt to be loaded with collectibles. There are a lot of small dealers who never have enough stock or time to open a shop. Paying a set-up fee once a week and displaying their wares at flea markets makes a lot of sense for these dealers.

There is a feeling of camaraderie and an attitude that antiques and collecting can be fun that I find exists among flea market sellers and buyers. This is missing at the big antiques shows where, unfortunately, the emphasis placed on the big-dollar items, the enormity of possible mistakes, the competition, and down-right hostility among some of the sellers have taken away the fun that used to exist.

It was inevitable that the climate would change. Collectors are being replaced by investors. At the larger shows, people rush from display to display. You reach for a piece only to have it pulled from your hands with the cry, "I saw it first!" Maybe it is an old-fashioned creed but I still believe that courtesy has its place. Even at flea markets, waiting buyers will swarm over a seller's truck, pulling merchandise from it before the driver is out of the cab. This is not all directed at retail buyers; dealers are the worst offenders. The competition for merchandise is fierce today.

The atmosphere is generally casual at flea markets, however. You have an opportunity to stand and have a cup of coffee with an old friend. Dealers get together for a few beers in the afternoon shade of a tent to talk over business. The potential buyer can ask about the collection of store tins and the seller will actually have the time to talk about them.

I've made it a point to set up at at least one flea market a year. It's worth it just to meet the retail buyers and make new friends. My pieces most of the time still all go to the dealers, and the best stuff always sells before ten o'clock. The dealers are invariably at a flea market early in the morning. Even with the hassle of packing the wagon the night before and getting up earlier than usual, setting up on the flea-market grounds is worth it.

The memories of great buys, the anticipation of selling out right down to the bare tables, freezing in the morning, baking in the afternoon; once you've done it, nothing quite equals it. Most dealers lug their lower-priced stock to the flea markets, but sometimes you will run into a real quality piece. If you like haunting the flea-market circuit, get there early and open your eyes.

It isn't hard to locate a flea market these days. If you're traveling on a Sunday and see a variety of campers and vans parked in a field, with card tables spread around, the odds are it's a flea market. Check the local papers. Look in the back section of the *Maine Antique Digest,* or *Arts and Antiques Weekly* put out by the *Newtown Bee,* Newtown, Connecticut.

The variety of collectibles displayed at flea markets is too vast to even start to list but it can be grouped into rough categories. You are sure to find some country items. "Country" means crude to some people but it doesn't have to be. Look for apple peelers, chopping bowls, baskets, storage boxes, quilts, etc. Remember that baskets, bowls, and other kitchen implements are still being made, so don't get stuck paying an antiques price for a new item. Check the paint on a piece of painted country furniture to see if it's new buttermilk paint. A lot of painted furniture turning up at flea markets these days is repainted. Look for signs of wear.

Beware the pristine basket; flea markets are where the majority of reproductions are sold. Expect any weather vane offered there to be a reproduction. Only a small number aren't. Unless you are absolutely sure of yourself, avoid the "bargain antique" in any field.

Most glass and china sold at flea markets is recent. Don't expect to fill in your collection of early Sandwich glass or Chinese Export porcelain from what you find there, but don't overlook it if it does show up. Occasionally it will. You will find pieces to add to that depression-glass collection and probably a hefty offering of Avon bottles. Flea-market merchandise is one place you can use that price guide to advantage. Most dealers price their stock pretty close to the prices listed, but not all do. If you're building a collection, you may find some pieces that fall way under the listing.

Over the years I've found the best bargains in the glass and china field to be ironstone china, ceramic tiles, and, strangely enough, sugar bowls. I've bought stacks of ironstone plates for under a dollar each, looked up the marks in a reference book, dated the plates, and turned a profit. The sellers of tiles often haven't checked the prices for new tiles at hardware or building-supply stores. Old tiles are worth at least as much as new ones. I don't know why so many sugar bowls gravitate into my hands. I've had salt-glazed English examples, marked Wedgwood pieces, and flow-blue ones. All at extremely low prices.

The paper collector will find happy hunting at a flea market. Big Little Books, The Bobbsey Twins and Hardy Boys series, catalogues, cookbooks — all types of paper show up. Avoid movie posters, Currier and Ives prints, and tobacco company ads unless you have experience with the originals, for these are being reproduced. An old frame doesn't mean anything. If the price is right and it fits your decorating need, then buy; but don't pay an exorbitant price for a reproduction.

Paper is an interesting field. Some collectors specialize in valentines, others in railroad timetables. Because it is such a large field the specialized collector can often do extremely well at the flea market. Few sellers take the time to research and accurately price their offerings.

I once bought an early Vermont cabinetmaker's diary listing his prices, offerings, paint formulas, day-to-day work details, and customers — for a dollar. That sort of diary or record is very scarce. It sold to a rare books dealer the same day. Another Sunday I saw a truckload of bound issues of *Harper's Weekly* sell for $40 and kicked myself all over the field because I didn't ask the price when I first saw them. The buyer showed me the full-page Thomas Nast Santa Claus drawings in the 1870-era Christmas issue. I wish he hadn't.

Old magazines don't show up in the quantity they used to, but at least a few will be for sale at most flea markets. Look for pre-World War II issues of *Fortune, Saturday Evening Post, Vogue,* and if you're extremely lucky, the French magazine *L'Illustration.* They have wonderfully framable advertisements. You can do your own decorating for a lot less than the price for finished pieces that the sellers charge. Actually, you should consider the possibility that anything you buy framed might have come from a magazine. Especially keep that in mind if you are offered magazine-size or smaller prints by Norman Rockwell, Maxfield Parrish, or other artists.

Flea markets sport offerings in other fields too. A friend of mine who collects antique auto parts and memorabilia haunts the local flea market. Rarely does a week go by that he doesn't find at least one addition to his collection. Hubcaps, speedometer cases, occasionally a radiator cap, sometimes antique garage-display cases, owners' manuals — he collects it all and sells what he can't use.

Another friend collects old radios and apparatus. I often see these two friends crisscross the field on the same morning, each lugging his treasures. Radios and automobiles have a lot in common. Anyone who collects in one of these fields usually knows a lot more about it than the seller. It's not uncommon to see either of my friends sitting down on the grass by a seller's booth delivering a little lecture on the intricacies of the item offered.

That's probably part of the appeal of collectibles. Once you've got the collection going you've learned enough about the subject that you do acquire some expertise. The dealer leans across the booth and points out the covered sugar bowl in depression glass and asks, "Isn't that a nice piece of Ruffled Florentine?" You murmur, "Yes, it's nice, but it's not Florentine; it's Royal Lace and I'll take it." Soon she's asking you to look at her other pieces. You talk about availability and local prices, and end up parting friends.

For a well-illustrated look at the field of collectibles the beginning collector may want to pick up *A Treasury of Nostalgic Collectibles* by Charles Jordan (Yankee, Inc.). The appendix of collectors' journals, magazines, and books could be especially helpful. Also highly recommended is *The Antique Trader Weekly,* published in Dubuque, Iowa.

Now let's turn to the new collectibles. By new I mean really new. I'm referring to collectors' plates, collectors' spoons, bells, etc. — all those objects that are manufactured specifically to be collected. Somehow I have a queasy feeling about these objects. They are mass produced. They are never meant to be used; nobody ever eats from a collectors' plate. Their only purpose in life is to be instantly collected. To me, there is something false about them.

Collectors' plates do go up in value, but I wonder how much of that increase is manufactured by the sellers. The collector has to stay in close contact with the sellers and manufacturers to know how many pieces are being produced, and where and when they are being distributed. If this is your field, I wish you luck. There is nothing I can say to help you.

Sometimes you'll find dealers looking down their noses at you when you mention your interest in the collectibles field. There is a tendency toward snobbishness in the antiques business. Try to ignore it. Think of yourself as an investor investing in tomorrow's antiques. Maybe I've given the impression that I have a bit of that snobbishness. If I have, I apologize. Collectibles are important. They are fun, too. If you like collecting and love your collection, that is all that is important. I love antiques. Some of those collectibles are going to be antiques one day. Maybe in a few years I and many other dealers will wish we had done the same collecting you are doing now.

Photo by John Harris

11

Saints and Sinners

AS you can probably tell by now, one of the most interesting facets of the whole antiques business is the people who work in it. Antiques have always drawn the oddballs, the one-off characters, the showmen and charlatans. A good friend of mine, former dealer now auctioneer, has summed it up this way: "Antiques is the only business I know of that has so many crazy people working in it. And once you're in, you can stay forever if you wish. You can do the job right up to the day you die."

You surely can. Many, many years ago I went to visit the ailing dealer Clifton Blake, who was spending his last days at a V.A. hospital in Vermont. Cliff, who in earlier years had worked in New York with those legendary glass dealers and authors, the McKearins, greeted me weakly. As we chatted he suddenly said, "Take a look under the bed." Among other treasures he had a pair of early cast-iron Hessian-soldier and-irons tucked down there for sale. When he passed away shortly thereafter, a lot of New England dealers acutely felt the loss. As much as Cliff was appreciated, he wasn't unique in his stick-to-itiveness. Many of the legendary old-timers do deal right up to their last days.

As a dealer I've found this association with such dealers to be especially rewarding. They operated back in the days when they were often the only person in an entire state who was selling something like folk art. In this day and age of lack of reverence for elders, it is unique to find a business that places a premium on experience and maturity but still welcomes youth to its ranks.

When passing through the Saratoga, New York, area, I used to make a point of stopping at the shop of a lovely lady who could have doubled for a Hollywood version of the typical grandmother. Typical, that is, until you got to know her. Barely five feet tall, pure white hair, she was a casting-office natural. Inside she was pure iron. Imagine a lady in her early seventies insisting she help you load into your truck a cast-iron wood stove weighing over two hundred pounds. And she did help, despite my protests.

She used to have wonderful surprises in her house. Rare Bennington foot baths, music boxes, great furniture, family portraits — everything came out of the area houses. She kept pushing me to meet her picker — a woman, which was un-usual because most are men — and one day I had the plea-sure. I couldn't believe my eyes. Her picker was every day as old as she was.

This lady told me of climbing up to the lofts of barns, and of manhandling big pieces of furniture down the stairs. It seems her approach, as a picker, was to call on her acquain-tances, sit through tea, exchange gossip, and mention her in-terest in antiques. Soon she was handling the family treasures and later she was buying them. Both ladies are gone now: God bless them, wherever they are. They were quite a pair.

Of course, along with the saints, the business has its share of sinners. Some are just slightly larcenous, others are out-and-out crooks. There aren't many like the dealer who pulled up in front of my shop several years ago. "Take a look at what I've got," he said. I followed him out to his wagon to view an amazing array of Oriental rugs and decorated crocks and jugs. "What kind of prices?" I asked. "Oh, they're all cheap, but you can't sell any of them in your shop," he replied. I knew what he meant.

Two days later he was in jail and the police were breaking up a fair-sized antiques theft ring. If he hadn't mentioned not selling them locally, I might have gotten into a lot of trouble. It's strange, but thinking back I wonder if he was just being naive or if he was testing me. Anyway, I'm glad I didn't buy from him. Dealers who stray over the line almost always get caught.

A different dealer left his mark on the business in another way. This guy used to flaunt his individuality in an outrageous manner. He'd show up at auctions as the archetypal Vermont farmer. Dressed in a ratty black coat, baggy wool pants, and floppy broad-brimmed hat, and wearing the most manure-laden buckle overshoes ever seen outside a cow barn, he'd stalk up to the auction crowd.

Fortunately for him, but unfortunately for the rest of the buyers, he had money to back up the costume. If he wanted something, he'd pay any amount for it. Consequently, he became the center of attention. Other dealers began to toady to him. You'd see him at the back of the tent surrounded by a ring of admiring, or fearful, dealers. Because of his buying power, auctioneers catered to his whims. They'd call out to him, tease him up another bid when some brave soul dared bid against him. If by chance someone did buck him, did walk away with something he'd wanted, he would stalk up to the offending party and demand they sell it to him immediately for a small markup. His threat was that if they didn't, they would never buy anything at any auction he attended again. From all I've heard he made good his threats.

This next story may or may not be true, but it has the ring of something that dealers would do to each other, so I'll tell it anyway.

A group of dealers had had it with this dealer's ways, let's call him Melvin, and decided to make some money from his outrageous habits. At one summer auction they carefully primed him. They mentioned that there was a great oil painting coming up at another auction a week hence. They also noted that another dealer, arch foe of Melvin, had said he was going to attend and get that painting. Melvin bristled. "He is, huh? Well, let's see him try!"

That auction turned into a real donnybrook. The rival dealer and Melvin fought over the painting all the way up to around $12,000. Melvin got it. He never knew that the rival dealer and the others met later and divided the money Melvin had paid for their painting, which they had purchased earlier for under $200. It was like shooting fish in a barrel.

If you attend many auctions, you will probably see a few of these little power struggles. Rarely will you find a dealer being set up as Melvin was, but you might witness a bidding battle between two rival dealers. Without being an insider you might not understand what's happening. Often the object being auctioned has nothing to do with the bidding. Two rival dealers have just decided to take out their animosity for each other in public. That it happens to be a chair or a rug on the auctioneer's block is incidental to the action.

If this happens, don't get involved in the bidding. The prices being realized don't bear any resemblance to the value of the object. Let the fools go. The consignor will be happy. So will the auctioneer. And above all, don't rush home and try to sell your similar antique for the price you saw at auction.

It is not only the professionals who provide the material for those oft-repeated stories about auctions. Just about every summer someone gets into trouble at an auction by not paying attention to what the auctioneer is selling. Crowds roar with laughter when the successful bidder stands in amazement as the auctioneer announces, "Sold! Fifty dollars each. Times six! Three hundred dollars for the lot!" "But, but — I thought I was bidding on the lot! Isn't fifty the price for the whole lot?" The auctioneer shakes his head sadly, "I said — if you had been listening, sir — that you bid so much a piece, and take the lot. Well, what are you going to do, take the lot?" The bidder glances at his wife, estimates the dent $300 will make in his checkbook, and shakes his head no.

Sitting down to the laughter of an amused crowd is not a pleasant experience, but it is bound to happen to anyone who doesn't pay attention at an auction. Sometimes the auctioneer is too busy to stop and re-auction the lot, so the winning bidder must take the goods.

Anyone who attends many auctions can tell similar stories. Sometimes it's the auctioneer who's the character. Take the auctioneer who used to throw half dollars into the box lots of junk in order to get a one dollar opening bid. Often the box had nothing of value beyond the two or three halves he would deposit there, but sometimes a few determined bidders would chase the box and its mysterious contents up to $4 or $5.

This particular auctioneer later developed the "if you

don't want it, I'll break it" technique. His auctions became the prime Saturday night entertainment for area residents. He'd buy a large number of foreign reproductions and state that, yes, they were reproductions, but since he was only asking such a low percentage of their value, they were bargains.

The audience would sit on their hands waiting for the act to begin. He'd beg for a bid, and then, seemingly giving up, state, "Well, if you don't want them, I'll break 'em." And he would; over his shoulder the plaster stein would go, to shatter into a thousand pieces upon the cement floor.

"Give me another!" he'd shout to one of his runners. They would protest and he'd demand they give him one, saying he'd break them all if he wanted to.

By now some of the weaker-hearted members of the crowd would be on their feet shouting, "No! No! I'll give you your three dollars!" Another voice would follow and the runners would be in the crowd passing them out as fast as they could.

Another local dealer and I used to attend his auctions because quite frequently he had real sleepers among his merchandise. His pickers would bring in some item that "Big Bill" didn't have any knowledge of or know how much it was worth. Waiting for these items to come up was a lengthy procedure, however. Often we'd wile away the time by retiring to a local bar until the loaves of bread, boxes of overripe fruit, and reproduction steins were disposed of.

Area people will long remember that cold winter night as we returned to the auction barn from our visit to the local pub only to find we were just in time for the if-you-don't-want-it, I'll-break-it routine. I don't know what happened to us, maybe it was the overheated hall, perhaps our resistance was low, maybe it was a combination of factors. We sat in the front row, right in front of "Big Bill." He begged and pleaded for a $3 bid for a plaster beer stein. Finally the first one went up and over his shoulder and crashed to the floor.

I think the other dealer yelled first, but maybe it was I. "Yes, yes! Break 'em. Do it!" The second stein was already in the air when our cries registered with Bill. No one had ever done this before. One of the runners, with a smile on his face, handed him another stein. It was like putting a clay pigeon into a skeet trap. As soon as it touched his hand, it was up in the air traveling in an arc to crash on the floor behind him.

Now the audience was coming alive: "No, no, don't break them!" But so were we: "Yes, yes, Bill! Go on, go on. Break the damned things! Yes, yes!" And we were yelling pretty loudly as I recall. It's a confession I don't like to make, but when excited, I can drown out almost everyone else, and the other dealer was about as good.

Bill was caught. The runners were having the times of their lives. Three pairs of hands were pushing steins at him, and he — well, he just couldn't stop his reflexes. Up they went, one after another, until two dozen plaster copies of German beer steins lay in shards on the floor behind a very confused auctioneer.

The place was a madhouse; everyone was buzzing. He managed to collect himself, glare at the runners, glower at us, and go on with business. He had no trouble getting bids, and prices were better than they'd been in weeks.

Later he told us, "I ought to ban you damn guys from my auctions, but you know, I had more fun doing that than anything I've done in years."

Auctioneers in general seem to be more interesting characters than the others one encounters in the business. They invariably develop into showmen during their careers. But certain dealers have turned into legendary characters too.

For years, several of us would frequent a certain junk shop on the New Hampshire-Vermont border. At least to everyone else it was a junk shop. But we knew those times when it wasn't. Ernie, the owner, ran his shop in a rather dilapidated building in a run-down section of town. Formerly a grocery store, it had a large plate-glass window through which one could look at piles of boxes, mounds of clothes, and stacks of books. Everything was exactly as he'd bought it. No repairs, no cleaning, no dusting. If something was in pieces when he bought it, that's the way you took it.

The first visit would usually discourage a retail customer.

But if you had patience and perseverance, shopping there could pay off. Ernie didn't price things; you had to ask. Poking into a pile of boxes under an overflowing table one morning, I found a small dome-topped pine chest. About eighteen inches long and perhaps ten inches wide and high, it was unusually heavy for its size.

Inside was the most fantastic variety of hand-blown bottles I'd seen. Miniatures, flasks, smelling bottles, medicine vials; all in a range of colors from amber to green to aquamarine. There were two Shaker Anodyne medicine bottles that were blown in a mold, from North Enfield, New Hampshire. I asked Ernie how much.

"I bought those up in Enfield. Pretty good lot, ain't it? Give me forty-five."

After being paid he winked and said, "Got to keep you dealers coming back. I only paid six dollars for the whole box, so I did OK, but not as well as you will!" He was right. I did all right, and I kept coming back.

Ernie was infamous for his buying trips. He'd take to the road for two or three days; where he went was a well-kept secret, but he'd tell us when we could expect him back. We would be sitting out there in front of the shop, heaters running in the winter, from seven o'clock in the morning on, awaiting Ernie.

His van would pull up and it was open season on antiques. Pulling chairs out of the back door with yells of "How much?", screaming "What's in the box under the sleigh?", we hardly gave Ernie a chance to shut his motor off.

Once a friend of Ernie's told us what it was like to go on a buying trip with him. "Ernie will never offer over a dollar for any chair. It's always take it or leave it and cash on the barrelhead. The damn fools almost always take it. He's got an uncanny sense of what houses to hit. We can be driving along this back road and we pass a likely looking farmhouse and I say, 'Let's stop here,' and he'll say, 'Nope,' and on we go to the next house, which looks too ritzy to me, and he'll say, 'Here,' and damned if he ain't right."

Ernie died a few years ago and a lot of well-known dealers

were at his funeral honestly mourning him.

Dealers have strange buying habits. Some will go into a shop and pick up the piece they want and walk around clutching it to their breast. Others look everything over before indicating that they are interested in any particular piece.

One of my favorites would carefully peruse my entire stock before he'd pick up some small inexpensive object and say, "What can you do on this?" I'd play the game and chop it to about half the sticker price. Immediately he would come back with questions about his price on the pieces he really wanted. I'd give him the standard dealer discount of from ten to twenty percent, depending on the item, and he would buy them all.

He rarely spent under $300 a call but that first item was the key. Helpers sometimes gave him the standard discount on the first item and he'd walk out without buying anything. It takes all kinds to make a world, and the antiques business is the place to find them.

Collecting antiques can be fun. Meeting fellow collectors, attending auctions, shopping at the big shows — these can be very rewarding experiences for a collector/investor. They can be safe experiences, too. The basic thing a beginning collector must do is study the field. Once you've read the books, seen and handled authentic examples, and reviewed the price structures, you are ready to begin buying.

You must remember, whenever you contemplate a purchase, that one unalterable law: if you have any doubts, any feeling whatsoever that a piece isn't right, you must obey that feeling and not buy the item. You may not know why the doubt exists, but if it exists at all, it must be obeyed. If you have done the research, if you are familiar with the antique, you will almost invariably find later that you were right in not buying.

Trusting yourself, that's what it comes down to. Have a reason for trusting yourself. The better dealers, the successful collectors and investors, all have this trust. You can have it too, but you must study. You must familiarize yourself with those items you want to collect.

You're going to meet dealers you can trust and like and a few you can't and won't. You'll experience auctioneers who are honest in their descriptions of pieces, polite to the crowd, and enjoyable to be around. You'll meet a few who you will swear last worked with the dirty-tricks department of the CIA. They won't last, though. You will listen to the stories of the great finds. Spring will find you itching in the harness waiting for the return of the outdoor flea markets. You will hoard your money for that one great auction coming up in two months. When the antiques journals arrive you will scream in rage if your spouse sets a cup of coffee down on them.

At cocktail parties, you will seek out the only other collector there and spend the rest of the evening discussing antiques, to the dismay of your partner. You might even get hooked to the extent of a friend of mine who can't manage to drive a car past a yard-sale sign. It doesn't matter what car he is driving — they all break down very conveniently at the least hint of a yard, garage, or lawn sale.

What's happened to you is very simple. You've joined the ranks of antiques lovers. Welcome. We're a distinguished group: ex-Presidents, industrialists, actors and actresses, literary people, robber barons, me, and now you. Have fun.

Photo by Neil Schaeffer

ABOUT THE AUTHOR

Native Vermonter David E. Hewett has been involved with the antiques business for some eighteen years, working at one time or another as a runner, a dealer, and a picker. Before that he was employed in an even wider variety of jobs, including production-line welder, vice president and board member of a natural-foods restaurant, and analyst in military intelligence.

Mr. Hewett has written articles for *The Washington Post, UpCountry, Leisure Magazine,* and *Maine Antique Digest.* He lives in Brattleboro, Vermont, with his wife, Janna, and is currently working on a novel about a religious community in Vermont in the 1870s, and a collection of short stories about the adventures of a detective who investigates the dirty tricks in the antiques world.